Glorious Lethal Euphoria

Radical Self-Mastery in a World Gone Soft

Written by Jack Sayler

Contents

Dedication

◈

*The rarest wealth is the people who
make you rich without money.*

To my circle of friends, colleagues, and mentors…your positive influence has shaped me in ways I could never have imagined. Your guidance, inspiration, and camaraderie have been a gift, teaching me the value of resilience, collaboration, and growth.

To Jim Thomas and The Mermen, I would love to claim your music as the soundtrack of my life.

To those whose examples showed me what I did not wish to become, I am equally grateful. Your lessons, though harder to embrace, were just as vital in forging my path.

To my father, whose wisdom to always choose the harder right over the easier wrong took time to sink in, but ultimately became my guide. Thank you for your enduring influence and counsel.

Above all, to my extraordinary wife, Linda, and our three incredible children, Kathleen, Jack, and Sam…you are my heart, my joy, and the most beautiful part of my life. Your love and presence are my greatest blessings, and this book is as much yours as it is mine.

With boundless gratitude and affection,

Jack

Preface

You must see yourself as a work in progress, never complete, never comfortable, always evolving.

I find the title of this book mesmerizing. I first saw these words, in this order, when I bought a CD named *Glorious Lethal Euphoria* written by an amazing band named The Mermen. The Mermen's cerebral instrumental psychedelic surf masterpieces almost immediately pulled me into a Zen-like need to discover the essence of human interaction and purpose. I found the phrase "Glorious Lethal Euphoria" a striking, poetic, and emotionally charged name that can be a great description of our lives:

Glorious - evokes awe, transcendence, higher purpose.

Lethal - suggests danger, intensity, edge; the cost or risk of true transformation and killing what's been harming you from the inside.

Euphoria - the peak emotional state, bliss, enlightenment, joy.

I consider this book almost as a manifesto for harnessing the beautiful brutality of life and rebelling against numbness through the art of self-mastery in a world that embraces division and distraction.

This is not another book about happiness, emotional cheat codes or hollow motivation. *Glorious Lethal Euphoria* is for those who refuse to drift through life and who know, deep down, that they were not born just to survive, but to reach their potential through developing the right mindset. If you're done blaming circumstances, your need for applause or fate for your worth, you're in the right place. Why write this book? I've lived on both sides. I've been disengaged, and I've been awake. I know what it's like to chase trophies and still feel empty, as well as what it means to build a life of fierce purpose from the inside out. I have found the lessons here are mostly carved from ancient wisdom, tested in modern struggle, and sharpened by my own failures and breakthroughs.

Why are these principles more urgent and relevant now than ever before? Because we are entering an era unlike any other. Artificial Intelligence (AI), automation, and relentless technological change are rewriting the rules of work, meaning, and identity faster than most of us can process. The world is getting louder, faster, and more unpredictable. AI will create jobs, destroy others, and force us to redefine what it means to be human.

Every day will bring new opportunities for joy and contentment, but also fresh temptations toward anger, anxiety, and distraction. Our character will be tested in ways we've never faced. What's right or wrong may feel less obvious, and the gap between what you can control and what you can't only widens. As AI and technology accelerate change, the core of being human, such as purpose, resilience and self-mastery, matters more than ever.

How are we supposed to deal with this tidal wave of stimuli and nonstop flood of news, noise, and uncertainty? Not with more hacks, more scrolling, or shallow optimism. But with a bedrock of non-negotiable principles and coping skills that don't change, even when the world does. That's why radical self-mastery is no longer a luxury; it's a survival skill. The world needs more authentic humanity. The one investment you can make that never depreciates is in yourself and who you become. That's what this book is about. Do not be surprised or alarmed to find some themes and phrases repeated several times throughout the book, as their repetition is designed to help readers internalize their significance. Glorious Lethal Euphoria was written to be your field manual for radical self-mastery.

My Influences

$\diamondsuit$

The Stoic Mindset

The Stoic movement began over 2,300 years ago, not in a palace or religious temple, but in the open marketplace of Athens under the *Stoa Poikile*, the "Painted Porch", where Zeno of Citium taught a philosophy forged not from comfort, but from crisis. After losing everything in a shipwreck, Zeno sought not pity, but purpose. From that seed of loss, Stoicism grew into a powerful framework for resilience, embraced by emperors and slaves alike. Its greatest minds, including Epictetus, a former slave who taught that true freedom comes from within; Seneca, a Roman statesman who wrote piercing letters on how to live and die well; and Marcus Aurelius, the Roman Emperor who journaled his private thoughts in *Meditations*, all showed that Stoicism is not a theory, but a practice. It teaches that we cannot control external events, only our judgments, actions, and attitudes. Driven by its core values - wisdom, courage, temperance, and justice – Stoicism offers timeless virtues that anchor us when the world spins out of control. Stoicism provides a path to sharpen us and offers a toolkit for clarity, calm, and character. It empowers us to meet adversity without complaint, to succeed without arrogance, and to love without attachment. Within its teachings are two of the most transformative ideas any human being can carry. The first being *Amor Fati - "Love of Fate"*, more simply put, to accept what happens is the beginning of peace. To love it is the mark of the wise. When Marcus Aurelius lost his children, when Epictetus suffered a broken leg and lifelong disability, they didn't curse the world. They didn't say, "Why me?" They said, "This, too, is for me." Amor Fati is the radical act of embracing every twist of life, not just as endurable, but as essential. As Marcus Aurelius said, "A blazing fire makes flame and brightness out of everything that is thrown into it." It's the leader who uses betrayal to grow stronger. The entrepreneur who loses it all and then builds again, better and smarter. Seeing heartbreak as redirection as opposed to ruin. When you love your fate, you stop resisting life and start collaborating with it. The second is *Memento Mori - "Remember You Must Die."* We often live like we are owed unlimited time. Memento Mori calls us back to the truth that our days are numbered. This should ignite us, not depress us. Seneca wrote, "You act like mortals in all that you fear, and like immortals in all that you desire." We procrastinate, postpone and hoard dreams for "someday." But the Stoics understood that tomorrow or someday is not promised. Marcus Aurelius reminded himself daily: "You could leave life right now. Let that determine what you do, say, and think." Memento Mori isn't about fearing death, but remembering to live, act, love, and serve in each moment. To live with *Amor Fati* is to embrace everything. To live with *Memento Mori* is to waste nothing. To live with both... is to live like a master.

Viktor Frankl

Viktor Frankl's book, *Man's Search for Meaning*, was carved out of unimaginable suffering. Viktor Frankl, an Austrian psychiatrist and Holocaust survivor, wrote it in just nine days after enduring years in Nazi concentration camps. He lost his parents, his wife, his brother, almost everything but his inner resolve. What emerged was a blueprint for human resilience, not just a memoir of unthinkable horror. Frankl observed that those who survived longest were not the physically strongest, but those who found meaning even in pain. He proposed that life is never made unbearable by circumstance, but by a lack of meaning and purpose. This became the foundation of Logotherapy, his school of thought that teaches man's primary drive is not pleasure, as Freud suggested, or power, as Alfred Adler claimed, but meaning. His message is simple yet seismic; we cannot always control what happens to us, but we can always control how we respond, and within that response lies our freedom. Frankl's work has become influential across psychology, leadership, and spiritual growth because it restores dignity to human experience. He maintains that life has meaning under all conditions, even the most miserable ones. Frankl's mindset offers a grounding truth that life is asking something of you. Your job is to answer, not with bitterness, but with courage, love, and responsibility. As he quotes in Man's Search for Meaning, "Those who have a why to live can bear almost any how." - Friedrich Nietzsche. That truth alone can transform lives.

Eckhart Tolle

Eckhart Tolle's *The Power of Now* is more than a book; it's a spiritual awakening disguised as words on a page. Tolle teaches mindfulness by gently dismantling the illusion that we are our thoughts about our past or future. He reveals the deeper truth that peace, purpose, action and power are only ever available in the present moment. While the past is memory and the future is imagination, life unfolds only in this breath and this heartbeat. When we are fully present, anxiety dissolves, because anxiety lives in the future. Guilt vanishes because guilt belongs to the past. In the present, we are no longer reacting to life but responding with it. Tolle teaches that the constant negative chatter in our heads, regret, fear, and judgment, isn't who we are at all. We are the awareness behind that voice. Once we realize this, we begin to experience a spaciousness within and a calm, alert stillness that becomes our greatest strength. Through the Power of Now, Tolle offers a radical invitation to return home to this moment, instead of chasing "somedays". As he says, "Realize deeply that the present moment is all you ever have. Make the Now the primary focus of your life." In that shift, everything changes, not outside you, but within you. And that's a key part of where your true transformation and self-mastery begin.

King Solomon

King Solomon's wisdom, recorded in *Proverbs* and *Ecclesiastes*, may have been written thousands of years ago, but it speaks to the modern world with enlightenment that transcends time. Solomon offers eternal principles grounded in truth, humility, and divine perspective. He understood the strengths, flaws and temptations of human nature, then addressed them with precise, poetic insight. In *Proverbs*, we find a guidebook for living wisely and effectively, such as working diligently, guarding your tongue, choosing your companions carefully, disciplining your desires and seeking wisdom as if it were a hidden treasure. These teachings are shockingly relevant today, as human nature has not changed. In *Ecclesiastes*, he pulls back the curtain on life's illusions, such as wealth, pleasure and fame, then declares that without meaning rooted in something greater than ourselves, all is "vanity." Yet he doesn't leave us in despair. His final call is profound: "Fear God and keep His commandments, for this is the whole duty of man." Solomon's ancient counsel reminds us what truly matters. His words cut through noise and trends to deliver timeless truth. No matter how advanced our world becomes, the human heart aches for wisdom, love, purpose, discipline, and meaning.

These visionary catalysts promote practical, not just theoretical, guidance as they help us manage the timeless thoughts that can inhibit growth in all aspects of our limited existence. While the landscape around us changes, emotions deeply embedded in our psyche from the beginning of time don't.

The sphere of human emotions, including fear, choice, meaning, insecurity, compassion, virtue, contentment, mortality, jealousy, etc., will forever influence human perception and perspective, providing no promises of overnight change or platitudes about "thinking positive." In Glorious Lethal Euphoria, you'll be challenged to confront fear, destroy excuses, master your mind, and rise, not for the world's approval, but for your own becoming and growth.

The life you and many others want won't be earned through inspiration but through radical self-mastery. This book is designed to reprogram your mental software. The journey ahead is necessary for those looking to maximize their existence on this earth. If you choose to keep reading, you are accepting a mission to become someone the world can't shake, and who honors their improbable existence with intention, grit, and glory. If you finish this book with greater discipline, deeper presence, more courage, and a clearer sense of who you are, you've found your own Glorious Lethal Euphoria.

"Once you realize the power of your thoughts, you won't just think anything. Once you realize the power of your words, you won't just say anything. Once you realize the power of your presence, you won't just be anywhere." - Emmanuel Acho

The Essentials

Chapter 1
The Universe Had to Get Everything Right

Human logic and reasoning are just not enough...

Our minds are both curious and constantly seeking explanations. How we came to be must be the purest and most basic sought-after answer we could ever seek, and that simple, unanswerable question contributes to life's beauty. Although science offers mechanisms, philosophy offers mental parameters, and religion offers faith and revelation, a concrete answer to why we are here either avoids us or leads to more and deeper questions.

Perhaps we were never meant to solve the existence secret, only to witness it. There is something profoundly human in standing before this mystery and simply saying, "I don't know, but I'm glad to be here." In that reverent uncertainty lies a deeper kind of truth...one that cannot be explained, only lived. Barring the consciousness of our being, let us dive into what the chances are for us to be born. Keep in mind, if you are reading this, you've already beaten astronomical odds. Let me show you why:

First, the universe had to exist. Science reports that the Big Bang occurred 13.8 billion years ago. If the expansion rate were even slightly different, no stars or galaxies would have formed. Massive stars then had to explode as supernovae, spreading fused hydrogen into heavier elements such as carbon, oxygen, and nitrogen. Then the laws of physics, chemistry, and biology had to emerge in such perfect balance for stars and galaxies to form. Among hundreds of billions of galaxies, the Milky Way had to gain shape with a stable solar system.

Secondly, the solar system had to be exactly right. Out of billions of stars in the Milky Way, our Sun formed with just the right mass, light, distance, and resilience. Then, the Earth had to form in a "Goldilocks Zone" with the perfect conditions for liquid water, a stable atmosphere, gravity, a magnetic field, and tectonic activity needed for life. That equates to one life-hosting planet out of trillions of worlds.

Thirdly, life had to begin and evolve. Somehow, non-living molecules on the early Earth assembled into self-replicating living organisms. This is still scientifically mysterious and mind-blowing. Over 3.5 billion years, life had to evolve through countless chance mutations and extinctions, as well as from single cells to human beings.

Fourthly, your ancestors all had to survive and reproduce. Every one of your ancestors, going back 4 billion years, as scientists say life began, had to survive everything from disease, famine, war, predators, and natural disasters. If any one of them had died young, not reproduced, or had chosen a different mate, you would not exist. The odds of this uninterrupted lineage are incalculably small. In addition, men release about one hundred to three hundred million sperm in just one ejaculation. Only one sperm can connect with one egg at one moment to create your exact DNA, a process that must be in perfect sequence down your entire ancestry line for your birth. If anything along the way happened a split second earlier or later, you would not be you; you would be a sibling, a different person, or nothing at all.

So, what does all this mean? It means your existence is a miracle of cosmic proportions! The universe had to evolve for billions of years, Earth had to support life, your ancestors had to live, and a once-in-all-of-history pairing of a specific sperm and egg had to occur just to produce you. Change any one of these factors, and your life wouldn't exist, let alone in an intelligent environment, another miracle. The chances of being born are more improbable than throwing a life preserver into any ocean and having a porpoise to strap it on. Your life is statistically impossible, and yet your existence proves the impossible is possible every day. This alone gives every human life profound weight, wonder, responsibility, and gratitude.

Dr. Antony Flew was one of the world's leading atheistic philosophers for most of his life. For decades, he debated and wrote books on why the existence of God, or any kind of design behind the universe, was simply not rational. Rational thought and scientific explanation were his only tools, and he wielded them masterfully. But something changed late in his life. After more than 50 years of insisting that everything must have a valid, empirical answer, Dr. Flew began to doubt the sufficiency of human reason. He watched as science uncovered more and more complexity in the origins of life and the universe. The more he studied the astonishingly precise conditions necessary for existence, from the fine-tuning of cosmic constants to the intricate machinery inside a living cell, the more he realized that logic alone was leading him to the edge of a great mystery. Flew's famous turning point came when he declared, "I now believe that the universe was brought into existence by an infinite Intelligence." He didn't become religious, but he admitted that the very existence of conscious, rational beings was so wildly improbable, so statistically impossible, that it transcended pure human logic. He said, "The most impressive arguments for God's existence are those that are supported by recent scientific discoveries."

Flew's journey shows that even the most rational minds can hit a wall where logic can only go so far. He accepted that the answers to life's biggest questions may be forever beyond our reasoning. And in that admission, he found a sense of wonder and gratitude he had never known before.

Tactical Tool: The Cosmic Lottery Meditation

While I sat on a park bench in Forsyth Park one afternoon, it hit me that the odds of me sitting right there, breathing that air, in Savannah, GA, on a sunny Sunday afternoon, watching a street performer juggle, along with a pigeon chasing a peanut, were astronomical. Billions of years of cosmic chaos and precision, every ancestor surviving by a thread, every decision led me here to this moment. The realization was dizzying as I began to realize that I have won the greatest lottery imaginable - existence itself. Use this reflection to anchor yourself in that truth:

1. What part of my life today feels most miraculous?

2. What specific action could I take today to honor the rarity of my existence?

3. How can I weave the spirit of this tool into the fabric of my day?

4. What thought, habit, or reflex could I release or reshape to embody it more fully?

5. How might living this truth sharpen my character and leave a deeper mark on the world?

Chapter 2
Wealth is Owning Moments, Not Things

*"The only true wealth is the profoundness
of the experience of your life."*

—Sadhguru

As we grow older and step deeper into our independence, life begins to demand more of us. The responsibilities get heavier. The challenges, whether in career, family, health, or relationships, become more complex. The real truth is that while life does not get easier, you can get stronger. You can train your mind, sharpen your focus, and condition your inner world just like you train your body. There are principles and mental frameworks that, once internalized, do not just help you manage life but help you master it. And I believe with everything in me, when you build the right mindset as your foundation, your life does not just become easier to navigate, it becomes profound and inspiring. It becomes a living example of what is possible, not just for you, but for those around you. Let us explore what this true wealth is and how you can build a life so meaningful, so mentally strong, and so deeply lived that it leaves a mark long after you're gone.

True Wealth Is Not Material...It's Existential

"Some people are so poor, all they have is money"—Peter Meagher. Material possessions, money, and status are tools that can provide comfort, but they are transient. Profound life experiences such as love, loss, and growth make connections at the core of a rich inner life, and those are what we remember on our deathbeds. In our last moments, we crave meaning and love, not money. While material possessions can be lost, devalued, or stolen, real wealth, such as wisdom, relationships, inner peace, and personal growth – resides within you.

Life's experiences become part of your story and can grow in value over time. You can revisit them, invest in them, reflect on them, and build upon them. True wealth is living a life that is deep, intentional, grateful, and fully felt. When you live with that mindset, money becomes a servant, not your master.

Experiences Expand Consciousness

Profound experiences are the true alchemists of the soul as they deepen our awareness and expand our perspective. Whether it is witnessing the birth of a child, hiking alone in silence, surviving personal tragedy, closing a hard-fought deal, or simply sitting still with your own mind, these moments stretch the edges of our consciousness. They interrupt the noise by peeling back the layers, and showing us something more essential about life, others and ourselves. Because once your lens on life changes, so do you. It shapes how you love with greater presence, how you lead with more wisdom, how you give with open hands, and how you live with clearer purpose. The wealth is not in the event itself; it is in the version of you that emerges from it. Profoundness deepens your awareness and perspective, with these experiences transforming how you see the world.

You Can Be Poor in Money but Rich in Meaning

Consumer culture equates wealth with accumulation, yet the rates of depression, burnout, and disconnection are at their highest. With the onslaught of Artificial Intelligence, one can expect those rates to increase unless managed through mastery of self. The antidote is presence, introspection, and living fully, not necessarily having more. History, literature, and real life are filled with examples:

- Viktor Frankl discovered that you can find meaning in suffering while in a Nazi concentration camp.

- Monks with no possessions radiate peace and contentment.

- Travelers and nomads often give up wealth for experience and never regret it.

- King Solomon, considered to be history's wealthiest and wisest man, found that one can have nothing material and still live a truly rich life with peace, wisdom, love, and moral strength.

- Marcus Aurelius learned that little is needed to make a happy life, as it is all within yourself and in your way of thinking.

Consider Re-orienting Your Life's Compass

As Socrates said, "The unexamined life is not worth living." Focus on realigning your goals from external achievement to inner richness by asking yourself:

- What moves me?

- What breaks me open?

- What moments feel eternal?

- Am I really living, or just existing?

- Did you love with your whole heart?

- Did you grow through your pain?

- Did you see beauty in the ordinary?

- Did you forgive when you could have resented?

- Did you wake up and say "thank you" for this breath, for this day, for this improbable shot at life?

Give yourself a wake-up call to live deliberately, and everything else will fall into place. You were not just born into life but chosen by the universe to exist, and that comes with responsibility. Not to be perfect, wealthy or impressive, although they may be byproducts of a vibrant and engaged life, but to live fully, squeeze meaning from every moment and live a life that leaves a dent in time, no matter how small. You owe the cosmos your effort to live intentionally...with gratitude, courage and wonder. Whether you are sweeping floors or leading nations, your experience is your legacy. Because in the end, the most successful life is not the one that had the most, it is the one that felt the most, loved the most, and meant the most. And that is a kind of wealth that no money can buy.

As a young doctor, Maria was driven almost entirely by achievement through grades, promotions, and recognition. But after her first humanitarian trip to a remote village, she found herself forever changed. Holding the hand of a dying child whose family had nothing but love to give, Maria experienced a depth of connection and awe that no academic award had ever touched.

The simplicity of shared laughter under starlit skies, the quiet dignity of elders, and the gratitude in each small gesture taught her to be fully present. Maria began to seek out these moments of meaning: hiking solo at dawn, journaling her inner life, and listening deeply to her patients' stories. She realized that the real wealth in her life came not from her title, but from the richness of experience and the expansion of her own consciousness. Those profound encounters became her true legacy, shaping how she loved, led, and lived from that moment on.

Tactical Tool: The Wealth Ledger of the Soul

After my parents passed, I sifted through the artifacts of their lives, photos, letters, clothes and other vestiges. They weren't just mementos, but proof of a life measured in love. I began to think of my children's laughter echoing down the hall, the fire of a sunset from my dock, the quiet joy of a fishing trip with old friends. I then understood this was wealth that is untouchable, unattainable and immune to time. From then on, I decided to count my riches in moments, not money. Use this reflection to anchor yourself in that truth:

1. What moment from this week will I remember when I'm old and why?

2. What small act could I take today to enrich my life's ledger with meaning?

3. How can I weave the spirit of this tool into the fabric of my day?

4. What thought, habit, or reflex could I release or reshape to embody it more fully?

5. How might living this truth sharpen my character and leave a deeper mark on the world?

Chapter 3
Response-Ability

"We always retain the ability to choose our attitude."
—Viktor Frankl

In the stillness between stimulus and response, there lies a sacred space that no man, prison, or trauma can rob from us. Viktor Frankl did not form this concept lightly. When he said, "We always retain the ability to choose our attitude," he spoke from the crucible of suffering itself, from inside the barbed-wire walls of concentration camps where dignity, identity, and humanity were systematically stripped away. And yet, he discovered something extraordinary. What Frankl observed was not just a coping mechanism, but a fundamental truth about human freedom. Circumstances, no matter how horrific, may constrain our bodies, silence our voices and bind our movements, but they cannot touch the inner realm of our will, mindset, or response. Attitude is the last of human freedoms.

Frankl saw men share their last crust of bread. He saw others give up and collapse into despair. The difference was not their surroundings, as they all lived under the same hellish conditions. The difference was internal. Some chose to remain kind, others bitter. Some chose purpose, others resigned. And in that, he discovered that between what happens to us and how we respond, there is a choice. And in that choice lies our growth and our power.

To retain the ability to choose our attitude means we are never completely powerless. You can lose your job, your health, and your loved ones. You can face betrayal, heartbreak, and injustice. But by possessing the capacity to say, "This will not define me. I will choose to grow, to remain compassionate, to keep my faith in life," then you are free. Not circumstantially, but spiritually, psychologically and existentially free.

Frankl invites us into this space of ownership. He challenges the modern tendency to forfeit responsibility for how we feel to what happens around us. We say, "They made me angry," or "This situation broke me." The truth is that no one makes us anything. They may act upon us, but we choose how to respond, and in that response, we can decide and show who we are.

Don't confuse this ability with denial or toxic positivity. It is about a conscious decision to own our perspective. When our external world crumbles, we can build an inner world of grace, courage, and meaning. Choosing our attitude does not always change the storm, but it changes us in the storm. Often, that is enough to rise above it. So, the question is not what will happen to you but who you will choose to be in the face of it? As Frankl taught the world, not even the darkest night can extinguish the light of a soul that refuses to surrender its freedom to choose.

The Power of Choice in Daily Life

It is one thing to embrace the idea that we can choose our attitude when we are reading a book in peace. It is another thing entirely when the car breaks down on a freezing morning, when your teenager hurls words that shatter your soul, when the diagnosis comes back positive, or when the business you have poured your life into begins to crumble. It's in these moments when the raw, unfiltered, inconvenient realities of life hit, that Frankl's truth becomes a lifeline. Let us bring this idea down from the mountaintop and into the grit of the everyday.

In the Workplace: You cannot always choose your boss, your coworkers, or your workload. But you can choose to approach each day with a growth mindset instead of a victim mindset. When someone takes credit for your work, you can respond with grace and keep building your excellence. If you are passed over for a promotion, you can use the setback as a stepping stone, not a tombstone. Those who rise highest in leadership are not always the smartest or most connected. They are the ones who consistently choose calm over chaos, composure over complaint, and solution over self-pity. That can be described as attitude in action.

In Relationships: Arguments will happen, and people will hurt you. Choosing your attitude means not letting anger or bitterness dictate how you respond, as you can pause, listen deeply then decide on your response. You can decide to communicate with clarity and respect, even when emotions run high. Choosing your attitude means being intentional and is far from being passive. You are recognizing that your reaction may shape the outcome far more than the original offense.

In Parenting: Parenting is one of life's most exhausting and sacred responsibilities. And it is easy to feel like you are failing. But attitude is contagious. If you respond to your children's mistakes with patience, if you model resilience when life gets tough, you are not just guiding them, you're training them to see life through a lens of strength and optimism. Frankl's principle is a reminder that how you show up as a parent is more powerful than what you say. Your chosen attitude becomes their learned behavior.

In Crisis and Loss: Perhaps nowhere is this idea more tested than in tragedy. The loss of a loved one or betrayal from someone close can leave us broken. Here, Frankl's words are not a dismissal of grief but become an anchor. Grief is not something to "get over." But even in the darkness, we can choose meaning. We can choose to honor a loved one's memory with the way we live. We can choose to find purpose in our pain and choose to heal, slowly, intentionally, and not let bitterness become our identity.

In the Mirror: Finally, the most life-changing application is personal. The voice in your head is the one you hear the most. Is it encouraging or defeating? Does it empower you or limit you? Each morning, before the world rushes in, you can choose an attitude of gratitude, presence, hope and action. You are telling the world, "I may not control everything, but I control me." That single decision, repeated day after day, is how lives are transformed. Choosing your attitude is not a one-time act of willpower. It is a daily return to your inner freedom and must become a practice. The more you choose wisely, the stronger your identity becomes, not as someone shaped by circumstance, but as someone forged by choice. That quiet superpower is available to us all.

During the chaos of Hurricane Katrina, Thomas, a lifelong New Orleans resident, found himself stranded on his rooftop for three days with his elderly mother, watching their neighborhood disappear under floodwater. Supplies dwindled. Heat and fear pressed in. Despair was everywhere, with neighbors screaming for help, helicopters circling but passing them by. Thomas could feel panic clawing at him, but he saw the terror in his mother's eyes and knew his response mattered. Instead of giving in to fear, he began telling her stories from his childhood, reminding her of everything they'd overcome together, and promising they'd see sunlight again. He waved at passing boats, shared what little water they had, and cracked jokes to keep her spirits up, even as the situation grew dire. Later, after their rescue, Thomas reflected that while he had no control over the storm, the rescue, or the losses, he never let the storm inside him win. Choosing hope each moment became his lifeline, and the memory of that choice became a quiet source of strength for the rest of his life.

Tactical Tool: The Sacred Space Between

Where I live, thunderstorms mean power outages. During one of these storms and outages, as I sat in my den, I began to intensely study a single candle burn—still air, frozen shadows, yet the flame danced. And I realized that no matter the storm, there's a place inside no wind can reach. You can't always choose what happens, but you can choose how you stand in its presence. That choice is quiet, and it's where you take your life back. Use this reflection to anchor yourself in that truth:

1. When was the last time I paused before reacting, and what did that pause give me?

2. What storm in my life right now is inviting me to stand steady rather than be swept away?

3. How can I weave the spirit of this tool into the fabric of my day?

4. What thought, habit, or reflex could I release or reshape to embody it more fully?

5. How might living this truth sharpen my character and leave a deeper mark on the world?

Chapter 4
Master the Helm and Any Sea Will Do

———————— ◆ ————————

Peace begins when you stop giving your energy to things outside your control. You can't direct the wind, but you can adjust your sails. Your thoughts, choices, and actions are another place where your power lives. If you seek peace, freedom and strength, learn first to divide all things in life into two categories: those within your control, and those which are not. This simple act of division, though quiet and invisible to others, is the foundation of a steady and contented life. Marcus Aurelius taught it not as a distant philosophy, but as daily practice and a shield against disappointment and needless suffering. His empire faced war, betrayal and plague, yet his mind remained anchored by this discipline.

What, then, is truly in your control? Your thoughts. Your judgments. Your choices. Your actions. Everything else, what others say, what others think, the past, and the outcome of your efforts, is not. Imagine for a moment standing in the middle of a storm, with the wind howling and the rain lashing against you. While you can't stop the storm, you can stand with your feet planted firmly. You can choose not to curse the sky, but you can choose your posture, breath and mindset. That is what Marcus Aurelius meant. The storm outside is not yours to command, but the storm within us is.

Most people waste their lives fretting over what they cannot shape. They twist themselves in frustration over the behavior of others, the unfairness of events or the twists of fortune. Realize all of that is noise. By focusing instead only on what is yours, your response, your attitude, and your effort, you become like a rock unmoved by the tide. The chaos around you does not find its way into your soul.

In practice, this means when someone offends you, you pause and say, "Their action is theirs and my response is mine." When the future feels uncertain, you tell yourself: "The future is not promised. My work today is what matters." When plans fall apart, you remember: "The plan was never guaranteed, but my resolve is within my power."

Marcus Aurelius understood this as a duty. To rule himself as carefully as he ruled Rome. We must follow his example in our own smaller empires like our families, our work and our inner lives. The secret is not to avoid hardship, but to carry yourself through it with clarity and grace. Again, focus only on what is within your control and let the rest pass like clouds across a wide and open sky. Marcus Aurelius wrote his *Meditations* in solitude, not for others, but as a reminder to himself. In the same way, we must remind ourselves each day through real, ordinary actions and directed thought.

At Work: You submit a project you've worked hard on. Your boss criticizes it unfairly. The outcome, whether they praise or reject it, is not in your control. But how you receive that feedback is. You can choose to listen calmly, apply what's useful, and let go of the rest. You control the effort you give, not the reward.

In Relationships: A friend stops calling, or a family member's version of events becomes inaccurate and disrespectful. You don't know why, and worrying, speculating or trying to control their feelings is wasted energy. What's in your control? Reaching out once, expressing kindness, and setting your own boundary. Then let it go and move on. You control how you show up, not whether they show up.

During Illness or Injury: Your body may fail you. Pain and limits come with being human. But even on a hospital bed, as Marcus Aurelius himself experienced sickness, you control your attitude. You control your patience and control whether you face it with bitterness or dignity.

With Money and Success: Markets rise and fall. Opportunities appear and disappear. You may lose money. But you control whether you remain honest, disciplined, and focused on long-term value instead of short-term fear. Fortune is not yours, but effort and integrity are.

In Traffic or Crowded Places: You're stuck in a line at a traffic light. The car in front of you won't move. Others become angry or impatient. Why should your peace depend on the pace of traffic? What is within your control is your breath, your patience, and your ability to use that moment for reflection or gratitude instead of agitation.

Facing the News and World Events: The world is filled with turbulence, such as politics, wars, and natural disasters…all things you cannot single-handedly control. But you can control what you consume, how much time you give to worry, and what actions you take locally. You control how much power you give to distant noise versus quiet focus in your own life. In every situation, pause and ask yourself: "What part of this belongs to me? What part belongs to fate?" Then invest all your energy into what is yours and release the rest. This is the practice of true freedom, lived in the rush of real days.

In the winter of 1812, as Napoleon's army marched on Moscow, Russian general Mikhail Kutuzov faced impossible odds. Supplies were scarce, morale was low, and the fate of his nation hung in the balance. The Tsar, his officers, and the people all clamored for bold action. Yet Kutuzov knew the weather, the enemy's ambition, and the coming winter were all outside his control. Instead of fighting for glory or bending to pressure, he chose a strategy of patient retreat, protecting his soldiers, conserving strength, and letting time and nature work as silent allies. He could not command the snow, the hunger, or Napoleon's pride. But he could control his discipline, his patience, his decisions. While others fretted and raged, Kutuzov stayed steady, refusing to let fear dictate his choices. In the end, the French army crumbled, not from battle, but from exhaustion and cold, while Kutuzov's peace of mind and self-mastery spared his men and saved his country. His legacy endures not because he controlled events, but because he mastered himself within them.

Tactical Tool: The Helm Within Gate

During the 2008 financial crash, a close friend's restaurant saw half of his regular customers disappear almost overnight. He couldn't control the economy, the stock market, or the layoffs hitting his city. What he could control was what came out of his kitchen and how people felt when they walked through his door. He doubled down on quality, greeted every guest by name, and started offering simple, affordable specials. Business didn't bounce back overnight, but the ones who still came in became fiercely loyal, and that loyalty carried him through. He couldn't change the storm, but he could set his own sail. Use this reflection to anchor yourself in that truth:

1. What in my life right now feels like the wind, uncontrollable, but still demands my steady hand at the helm?

2. Where am I spending energy on the tide instead of my sails?

3. How can I weave the spirit of this tool into the fabric of my day?

4. What thought, habit, or reflex could I release or reshape to embody it more fully?

5. How might living this truth sharpen my character and leave a deeper mark on the world?

Chapter 5
"Do Not Fear" - The Universal Command

Ralph Waldo Emerson's quote, "Fear defeats more people than any other one thing in the world," reverberates so clearly throughout mankind. Across every era, in every culture, and through every wisdom tradition, one message rings out above all others: "Do Not Fear." This isn't just helpful advice, but an edict and universal imperative repeated by sages, philosophers, prophets, and spiritual masters who understood the real enemy of the human spirit. Why is "Do Not Fear" the most repeated phrase in the Bible? Why does it echo in the meditations of Stoic emperors, the calm teachings of the Buddha, the riddles of Zen masters, and the proverbs of wise elders? Why do leaders and liberators, from Moses to Martin Luther King Jr., urge us to let go of fear? Fear is humanity's oldest, most cunning adversary, and it will most certainly always be. Long before the first written word, fear was etched into our biology as a survival mechanism. But as civilization advanced, that instinct, while once a guardian, became a warden. Today, it isn't fate that traps us, but fear. It locks us in invisible prisons of hesitation, self-doubt and regret. The wise have always recognized this:

- "Of all the liars in the world, sometimes the worst are our own fears." —Rudyard Kipling.

- "Fear is the main source of superstition, and one of the main sources of cruelty. To conquer fear is the beginning of wisdom." —Bertrand Russell.

- "He who is not every day conquering some fear has not learned the secret of life." —Ralph Waldo Emerson.

Wherever there is stagnation, avoidance, or resignation, fear is the architect. Self-mastery means breaking those chains. Fear distorts reality by making threats seem larger, possibilities seem smaller, and the present moment feels suffocating. When fear rules, reason is exiled, and vision narrows to a pinhole.

Fear has proven to corrupt judgment, breed conflict, and poison the heart. It keeps us resisting change and doubting our worth, as well as driving cruelty, envy, and division. Why is fear so universally opposed? Because it is the antithesis of faith, not just religious faith, but faith in life, purpose, love, and ourselves. In scripture, angels and prophets greet the uncertain with, "Fear not." The Bhagavad Gita urges, "Abandon all fear and arise." Where there is fear, the soul shrinks. Where there is courage, however trembling, life rushes in.

Every tyrant knows to control people, sow fear. Every liberator knows to awaken them, remove fear. History is a centuries-long struggle to be free—politically, socially, spiritually. The founders of every revolution had to conquer fear within themselves before they could free others. The wise choose to simply refuse to be slaves to imagined catastrophes, rumors or threats. Self-mastery isn't about never feeling fear but about recognizing it, learning from it, and choosing to move anyway. Seneca wrote, "We suffer more often in imagination than in reality." Viktor Frankl saw, even in the camps, that those who found meaning, even in suffering, could transcend fear and despair.

When fear is put in its place, we become free to practice the important virtues like courage, love, justice, generosity, wisdom and presence. None can flourish while fear is in command. "Do Not Fear" is not wishful thinking, but the hardest discipline. The line between a life survived and a life transformed is the decision to face fear not as a master, but as a messenger. Fear only ever points to what matters most. Meet fear with the mentality that "I am not yours to command." Step through this gate, and every other path opens.

But how do we live "Do Not Fear" in today's world, where threats are relentless, both real and imagined? Most of us aren't facing lions in the dark or swords at dawn. We face subtler but equally paralyzing fears like the fear of failure, judgment, being left behind, being found out, losing our chance, or never measuring up. Today's fears come as what-ifs, silent doubts and silent shame. Fear's faces have multiplied, but its goal is to keep you small, safe and never fully alive.

The truth is, everyone feels fear, even the strongest and wisest. The difference isn't the absence of fear, but the decision to act while fear is present. Think of the entrepreneur betting everything on a new idea, the artist bearing their soul in a painting, or the soldier stepping forward in a heated battle. None is fearless, but they are committed to something greater than their fear.

You're not born into this life without danger or uncertainty. But you can respond to them with wisdom, courage, and action. Self-mastery forces you to acknowledge there may be fear, but you just don't let it dictate your story. The next time fear shows up in your world, remember fear's presence isn't a prophecy, then turn it into an invitation and an opportunity to master it.

When you mentally replay the worst-case scenario, your mind believes it's real. Your heart races, breath quickens, muscles tense and logic is often lost. Suddenly, you're not truly living and become imprisoned in a future that hasn't even happened, and then, even a small step feels impossible. Keep in mind that if repetition can build fear, it can build courage too. If fear is just a script, you can choose to write a better one. Imagine yourself speaking and being heard, leaping and landing, failing and rising.

The mind can't always tell the difference between what's imagined and what's remembered. If you can rehearse disaster, you can rehearse triumph. The true battlefield is not out there, but within. The moment you stop letting fear narrate your story, you reclaim your power, and you don't have to feel brave to act brave. You don't need certainty to move forward; you just must stop letting fear have the loudest voice.

That voice is persuasive, but it isn't always true. Fear's greatest lie is that it defines your limits. Fear is just a signal that you've reached the frontier of your growth. What you do at that edge shapes your life. Most people miss this:

- Fear grows in silence, darkness, avoidance, and delay.

- The more you run, the bigger it becomes.

- The more you try to outthink it, the louder it shouts.

- Fear doesn't shrink with time. It shrinks with exposure.

Your brain is obsessed with safety, avoiding risk and not geared toward self-mastery. Your brain can be your greatest ally, but only when you train it, not when you blindly trust it.

Mark was a mid-level sales manager for years, always just missing the company's top tier. He worked hard, knew his industry, and watched others, some less experienced, pass him by for promotions and big accounts.

He told himself, "It's luck, or office politics, or maybe I'm just not cut out for leadership." But the truth nagged at him. Every time a major opportunity came up—a new client, a speaking engagement, or a shot at a management role—he found himself procrastinating, hesitating, making excuses. One day, during a workshop, the facilitator said, "Most people are not held back by talent or resources, but by the fear they won't admit. What fear is running your life?" That question hit Mark like a brick. He realized he wasn't afraid of failing, but his fear was of looking foolish, being criticized, stepping into the spotlight and falling short. His "comfort zone" was a prison built out of what-ifs. For the first time, he wrote it down: "I am afraid people will think I'm a fraud." That simple act, naming the real fear, changed everything. The next time he felt the urge to shrink back, he remembered: "This isn't fate or lack of ability. This is just fear trying to run my life." So, he volunteered to present at the next big sales conference. He was nervous, he stumbled over a few lines, but he delivered, and the crowd responded. He asked for the big account he'd always dodged. He started small, but the momentum built. Within a year, he was the company's top performer, not because he was fearless, but because he finally saw fear for what it was: a liar, not a leader. Growth begins the moment you admit what you're afraid of. Most limitations are fear in disguise. Once you call it out, you reclaim the power to act anyway, and that's when everything starts to change.

Tactical Tool: The Fear Gate

A buddy of mine was learning to surf big waves in Santa Cruz, California. As we sat in the lineup, a big set rolled in, and he froze. The waves towered over him, and his heart was pounding so hard he could hear it. He wanted to paddle back to shore, but his surfing mentor yelled, "Go now!" He went. The wave smashed him, tumbling him underwater until he didn't know which way was up. But when he surfaced, gasping, he realized the thing he'd feared most had already happened, and he was still there. The next time a big wave came, he paddled straight into it. Fear was still in his chest, but it no longer had the final say. He felt something deeper than exhilaration…he felt free. Not from danger, but from fear's grip. Use this reflection to practice stepping through your own gates:

1. What fear is quietly shaping my decisions right now?

2. What possibility might be waiting on the other side of that fear?

3. If fear is just a signal, what is it pointing me toward?

4. What small, deliberate action could I take today to lean toward the thing I fear instead of away from it?

5. How might choosing courage here ripple through the rest of my life?

The Essentials Review

We have started with the Essentials as an unbreakable foundation. The guidance set forth in the following chapters is written to refine it. As we continue this journey toward self-mastery in your life, I invite you to pause for a moment and reflect on the profound insights shared in the previous five chapters. These ideas are not merely thoughts to read and forget, but principles to be lived, breathed, and woven into the very fabric of your mind and heart. True self-mastery begins with deep integration of these long-standing truths. No matter the world we inhabit, these fundamental principles remain our unshakable bedrock. Let's take a moment to recap what you must truly internalize:

Be deeply aware of the miracle that is your existence: To truly live is to recognize that simply being here, in this vast cosmos, at this precise moment in history, is nothing short of miraculous. You are not a cosmic accident in time and space, nor a mere bystander in the story of life. Your presence is a rare and extraordinary gift, a beacon of something far greater than yourself.

Understand that true wealth is not found in gold, possessions, or fleeting achievements: True riches lie in the profoundness of your experience, like the joy that fills your heart, the lessons carved by struggle, and the wisdom born from moments both grand and subtle. This is the treasure that endures beyond the reach of time and circumstance.

Embrace your ultimate freedom: The power no one can take from you is your response. Life will throw countless challenges in your way, many beyond your control. But in every moment, you hold the sacred power to choose your reaction and the meaning you attach. This sovereignty of spirit will shape your destiny.

Focus your time and effort on what is in your control: Stoicism reminds us that peace comes from focusing only on what lies within our power. Let go of worries over what you cannot change. Anchor your energy in what you can command, including your thoughts, your actions and your attitude.

Do not fear: Focusing on fear, once vital for survival, becomes a prison when left unchecked, locking us in hesitation, self-doubt, and regret. Every spiritual and philosophical tradition warns that fear keeps us from our highest possibilities. The great teachers urge us to let go of fear because only then can courage, love, and wisdom take root and flourish. A liberated life begins where fear ends.

The chapters ahead will help put you on the path to owning your story, commanding your emotions, and aligning your actions with your highest values. Remember, true mastery is not about perfection or control over external events; it is about unwavering control over your inner world. When your spirit is anchored in truth and your will is aligned with purpose, no obstacle can derail you. Prepare yourself to embrace discomfort, question old beliefs, and commit fully to the process of becoming. Self-Mastery is not a destination but a dance between intention and action.

Shaping Thought

Chapter 6
The Constitution of You

"First say to yourself what you would be,
and then do what you have to do."

—Epictetus

A deliberate creed of non-negotiables is baseline equipment when facing the distractions, temptations and contradictions we wade through in daily life. What is a creed of non-negotiables? It is a deliberately crafted declaration of the principles, standards, and boundaries you refuse to compromise on, regardless of the pressure, conditions or circumstances. It functions as a compass because it directs your daily choices toward your highest values, and a shield guarding you from drifting into mediocrity, conformity, or self-betrayal. It's that line in the sand that says, "This is who I am, this is where I stand, and this is where I'm going, regardless of the noise around me." We are constantly fed diluted identities with endless content and reasons to trade our deepest calling for temporary satisfaction. This is why having a creed is critical, as it's an act of defiance against mediocrity.

You need a creed to have as an immediate reminder of self when your emotions falter and your mind looks for an escape. It won't ask for your mood or succumb to your excuses but it is designed to call up your highest standard and prompt you to rise to it…even when everything inside you wants to stay small. Committing to a creed speaks to the spiritual and psychological confusion directing us, and that many of us are silently fighting. See the Glorious Lethal Euphoria Creed below:

The Glorious Lethal Euphoria Creed

I am not here to survive.
I am here to become.
I'm not who I was yesterday.
I'm who I decide to become right now.
I was born with impossible odds.
I honor that by living with impossible intention.
I reject comfort disguised as safety.
I destroy excuses wearing the mask of logic.
I silence the voice that says, "Maybe later."
My mind is my weapon.
My will is my compass.
My soul is my fire.
I will not outsource my purpose.
I will not wait for permission to rise.
I will train my thoughts.
I will choose my attitude.
I will guard my circle.
I will speak truth—first to myself, then to the world.
I will be both lion and lamb: fierce and full of grace.
I am the miracle. I am the discipline.
I am the Glorious. I am the Lethal. I am the Euphoria.
And this is not motivation.
This is war for my soul.

The opening lines of the Glorious Lethal Euphoria Creed, "I am not here to survive. I am here to become," are an immediate rejection of passivity, especially when survival is praised and

41

safety is sold as the ultimate virtue. This directive steps you into transcendence. It flips the script on comfort and exposes its true nature. Lines like, "I reject comfort disguised as safety," and "I destroy excuses wearing the mask of logic," cut through the mental gymnastics we perform to justify playing small. We've mastered the art of rationalizing our stagnation and we require radical accountability. Excuses, no matter how intelligent they sound, are still barriers to becoming who we're meant to be.

One of the most profound declarations, "I will not outsource my purpose," is more than a sentence; it's a philosophy. We can't look to others to hand us meaning; we must create it and own it. Don't wait for permission to live fully, just take it. There is brilliance in its integration of duality. "I will be both lion and lamb: fierce and full of grace." The line offers the commitment to strength tethered to wisdom and power anchored in peace.

Lastly, "This is not motivation. This is war for my soul" is the line that separates every other pep talk or affirmation floating online. Motivation fades, and life can get heavy, but a war for the soul? That's a lifetime commitment that places your self-mastery at the highest possible stakes. You are now playing for the quality of your being, not just achievement. It's armor for anyone willing to live awake, alert, and aligned. When the world is pulling you outward, like gravity, your creed pulls you back inward into your will and becoming.

Admiral James Stockdale was a U.S. Navy pilot shot down during the Vietnam War. For over seven years, he was held as a prisoner of war in the infamous "Hanoi Hilton," enduring unthinkable torture, isolation, and psychological warfare. The camp was designed to crush the human spirit, rattle the mind, numb the heart, and destroy identity. Many prisoners broke. Some died. Yet Stockdale not only survived, he became a leader, and a light for the other men, also held captive.

Stockdale had a personal creed, a non-negotiable code he wrote and lived by before his capture, rooted in his study of Stoic philosophy and the conviction that every man is responsible for his own soul. He refused to let his captors define him or break his core values. His internal compass was clear, even as the world around him spun into chaos. Stockdale's personal creed included:

- *"I will never lose faith in my ability to prevail, no matter the darkness."*

- *"I will never confuse faith that I will prevail in the end with the discipline to confront the brutal facts of my current reality."*

- *"I will not betray my fellow prisoners or my country, regardless of personal cost."*

- *"I am responsible for my reactions, even if I cannot control my circumstances."*

This creed was not motivational fluff. It was armor. When motivation faded, when pain made thought itself a battle, his creed did not ask for his mood. It did not make room for his excuses. It reminded him, even at his lowest: You are not here just to survive. You are here to become.

The impact: *He led covert resistance inside the prison, creating systems of communication and morale. He helped fellow prisoners withstand torture by teaching them the importance of holding on to a line in the sand, what you will and won't give up, no matter* *the cost. When he was paraded before cameras, instead of cooperating, he disfigured himself so he could not be used for enemy propaganda—risking further torture but refusing to betray his code. Stockdale later said that those who survived the camps were not the most optimistic or the strongest physically, but those with a creed had something inside them that could not be negotiated, broken, or bought.*

Tactical Tool: The Non-Negotiable Compass

My most trusted mentor, without warning, once slid a blank sheet of paper toward me and said, "Write down the ten things you will never compromise on, no matter the cost." My mind leapt to vague ideals like honesty, loyalty, and perseverance. But he shook his head and said, "Not what sounds noble, but that you will actually live or die by." I stared at that paper for hours, until the words came, not as pretty slogans, but as non-negotiable battle lines. Use this exercise to forge your own unshakable creed:

1. What are the top five values or principles I would never trade, even under pressure, threat, or temptation?

2. How would my life change if these were not just ideals but laws I lived by?

3. Which of my current habits, relationships, or decisions violate my own code, and what will I do to correct them?

4. What single line could serve as my personal "battle cry" when my resolve is tested?

5. How will I remind myself of this creed daily, so it becomes a reflex rather than a wish?

Chapter 7
Your Voice is the Architect of Your Mind

---◆---

Many people believe that the path to success or fulfillment is about chasing bigger opportunities, more visibility, or working harder than the person next to them. That's natural, as we've been conditioned to think and see success in terms of hustle, rewards, and recognition. It's about recognizing that the true treasure is not out there. It's the lost parts of yourself and a union with the deeper, sacred forces that live within you and beyond you. It's the thing every culture once knew as Spirit, and with that, you become "next level" in anything you do or want to do.

Real mastery doesn't begin with what's outside you. It begins with having the courage to turn inward. Often, what we think we want, wealth, status, the perfect relationships, are just entry-level reflections of something deeper we're missing. Beneath all that is a quieter truth, and the real work is facing yourself. It's the honest, sometimes uncomfortable process of understanding your patterns, your fears, and the parts of yourself you've ignored or hidden. This kind of work doesn't happen on social media or on a balance sheet. It happens in the quiet moments of reflection, in stillness, in solitude, or through trusted guidance. And when you do this inner work, the reward is not just external success. The real treasure is recovering the parts of yourself that felt lost; your clarity, your peace, your purpose. It's the kind of success no one can see, but everyone can feel when they're around you.

The Silent Conversation That Shapes Your Life

It's a fact that many overlook that the most influential voice in your life isn't your boss, your parents, or even your closest friends. It's the one voice only you hear…your own. Science calls it self-talk. Psychologists call it inner dialogue. Whatever name you give it, research consistently shows that self-talk shapes not just your mindset but your actual outcomes.

Studies from Cognitive Behavioral Therapy and sports psychology alike demonstrate that individuals who consciously practice positive self-talk enjoy higher resilience, stronger problem-solving abilities, and even better physical health.

The words we speak, both out loud and in silence to ourselves, are incredibly powerful tools lodged in our self-mastery arsenal. The language we use isn't just a reflection of thought; it shapes thought. The brain doesn't really care what is true; it only cares what you repeat and the story you tell yourself. By changing your words, you can change your life.

Neuroscience has proven that every complaint rewires your brain like trauma, and just 60 seconds of negative self-talk changes chemicals in your mind to strengthen fear pathways. Self-talk doesn't announce itself as dangerous, but it creeps in as humor, casual sarcasm, or reflexive statements like, "I'm so stupid," or, "That's just my luck."

Even when said jokingly, the brain does not process sarcasm as separate from reality. Neuroscience confirms that repeated phrases, whether spoken in jest or frustration, create neural pathways that reinforce those beliefs. To put it simply, if you call yourself worthless often enough, your brain will start to believe it, adjust your behavior, expectations, and even your stress hormone levels accordingly. That's why it's critical to eliminate negative self-talk entirely, not just reduce it.

Every time you put yourself down, you're watering weeds instead of flowers in your mental garden. When you say, "I can't," or "I always screw this up," you're handing your subconscious a script to follow. Self-mastery begins with taking responsibility for that script. If you wouldn't let a stranger speak to you that way, why allow yourself?

On the flip side, intentional positive self-talk is not delusion, but it is a discipline. Words like "I'm learning," "I've got this," "I can figure it out," or "Every challenge is an opportunity" may feel unnatural at first, but like exercise, the effects build over time.

As Muhammad Ali famously said, "I am the greatest. I said that even before I knew I was." This isn't arrogance. It's programming. Your words set the boundaries of your reality. A few words and phrases I encourage you to make staples in your inner dialogue:

- I am capable.

- This setback is a setup for a comeback.

- What am I learning from this?

Consider also these quotes as mental guardrails:

- "Whether you think you can, or you think you can't, you're right." —Henry Ford

- "Be careful how you speak to yourself. You're always listening." —Unknown

- "Affirmations are not wishes; they're instructions." —
Louise Hay

Speak to Connect—The Power of Inclusion Over Exclusion

If self-talk shapes your inner world, the words you use with others do more than reflect that world; they reinforce it and determine how others perceive you. One of the most overlooked yet quietly transformative shifts in self-mastery is becoming intentional about using words of inclusion rather than words of exclusion.

In their book, *In the Zone,* Perry and Jamison draw a clear line between the two. Inclusion language fuels momentum, while exclusion language undermines it. One can describe inclusion language as candid, positive, and empowering, a tone even children instinctively use when they say, "It was great!" Simply put, people gravitate toward those who make them feel part of something. Inclusion language invites connection with words like we, us, together, let's, and our.

Exclusion language, on the other hand, is the vocabulary of doubt, absence, omission, equivocation, and diminution . . . the language of hesitancy, anxiety, and fear that tells you what isn't, couldn't, shouldn't, can't, and won't. Have you ever noticed there are some people in your life that you really don't enjoy talking with, or seem to be negative people, but are not sure why? Nine times out of ten, their language is covered with words of exclusion. Maybe they don't enjoy speaking to you for the same reason, so pay attention to your words as well.

Research in organizational psychology shows that leaders who unconsciously use exclusionary language are consistently rated lower in both competence and warmth, two pillars essential to influence. In every domain, including business, leadership, family and friendship, the words you choose can be the bridge that brings people closer or the wall that keeps them out.

We withdraw from those who make us feel shut out. Inclusion-based language invites others in. Compare: "You guys need to figure this out," versus "Let's work through this together." The first distances. The second builds trust. One positions you as an outsider looking down; the other as a leader standing beside. Regardless of your audience, this distinction directly affects how credible, likable, and trustworthy people perceive you to be. Exclusion-based language does the opposite.

Why does this happen? It comes down to basic human wiring. As tribal creatures, our brains are constantly scanning for cues like…Am I safe here? Am I valued? Do I belong? Every word we hear helps answer that question. When your language signals inclusion, it elevates not just your personal brand, it elevates the room you're in. You become a unifier rather than a divider. And in environments where trust and influence matter, being a unifier is invaluable. At a televised press conference in November of 1973, President Richard Nixon, while under scrutiny for his role in the Watergate fiasco, famously declared, "I am not a crook!" Imagine if he had instead declared, "I am an innocent man!" Although both statements are basically saying the same thing, one comes across as more positive and trustworthy. More examples:

- "I feel good," instead of "I can't complain."

- "I'm pleased," instead of "I couldn't ask for more."

- "Let's do it," rather than "I don't see why not."

One of my favorite reminders comes from Maya Angelou: "People will forget what you said, people will forget what you did, but people will never forget how you made them feel." Inclusive words make people feel seen, respected, and valued. Exclusionary words make them feel invisible. Self-mastery isn't just about how you treat yourself. It's about how your presence shapes the experiences of others. Master your language, and you'll master connection. That is how influence grows from the inside out, and from word to word.

Tiger Woods, once the most dominant golfer in the world, saw his life unravel in front of millions. Between 2009 and 2017, he endured public scandal, career-ending injuries, chronic pain, multiple surgeries, and humiliating personal losses. The world that once cheered his name now doubted he would ever win again—if he could even walk the course. But behind the scenes, something powerful was happening. Tiger wasn't just training his body—he was rebuilding his mind, word by word. In countless interviews and his own memoir, Woods described a turning point not on the green, but in his inner dialogue. At his lowest, his self-talk was toxic: "I'm done," "I'll never come back," "Everyone is right about me." These phrases, spoken in anger or despair, fueled more pain and self-sabotage. He noticed that every time he repeated them, even as jokes, he played worse, healed more slowly, and felt less worthy of fighting for himself. Aided by therapy, coaches, and meditation, Tiger learned to guard both his inner and outer speech. He started intentionally changing his self-talk:

- ***Instead of:*** *"My body is broken," he said, "I'm learning how to play a new game."*

- ***Instead of:*** *"I'm a failure," he said, "Every setback is data. I can improve."*

- ***Instead of:*** *"No one believes in me," he told himself, "I know who I am. I know what I can do."*

It didn't happen overnight. There were relapses and bad days, tough weeks, moments where the old tape played. But as he practiced, those intentional words created new grooves in his mind. With every positive statement, he built a new internal environment that allowed for growth, resilience, and even joy. Against all odds, in 2019, at age 43 and after 11 years without a major win, Tiger Woods won The Masters again. The world called it "the greatest comeback in sports." But Tiger himself said the real victory wasn't the trophy, it was reclaiming his own mind. He said, "The hardest battle was the one in my own head. Learning to be kind to myself, learning to speak to myself as I would a friend— that's what allowed everything else to change." Tiger's comeback was not just about golf; it was about self-mastery through self-talk. He is living proof that your words create your reality. If you repeat defeat, you'll find evidence for it everywhere. If you repeat resilience and learning, you program your mind to look for—and act upon—opportunity, growth, and healing. It's not magic; it's neuroscience. You are, quite literally, building new neural pathways and laying new tracks for your life. Tiger's journey shows: Guard your inner and outer speech because your soul truly becomes what it repeats. And here's the ripple: Tiger's comeback didn't just inspire him. It inspired millions to believe in second chances, to speak differently to themselves, and to reclaim lost parts of their own story. His transformation happened first in his mind with words no one heard but him.

Tactical Tool: The Speech Audit and Upgrade System

Years ago, I caught myself saying half-joking but half-serious, "I'm terrible at remembering names." It seemed harmless, but I started to realize I'd been saying it for years, and the pattern became clear: I *was* terrible at remembering names. Not because I couldn't, but because I had been telling my brain, over and over, "This is who you are." I'd been building this mindset out of my own words and living in it without question. That day, I tried something different. I replaced the phrase with: "I'm getting better at remembering names." I said it every time I met someone new, even if I still forgot a name moments later. Weeks later, I noticed the change, not just in my memory, but in my mindset. I had stopped reinforcing the lie that I couldn't improve. I was laying new tracks in my brain. That's when it hit me: My words were not just describing my reality, but they were building it.

Here's how to rebuild yours:

1. **Run the 24-Hour Audit**—For the next day, track *every* negative phrase you say about yourself, out loud or in your head. Don't judge. Just collect the data.

2. **Name the Repeat Offenders**—Identify the top three self-sabotaging statements you repeat most often.

3. **Write the Antidotes**—For each, create a short, positive replacement statement that feels believable and actionable (take "I can't do this," and change to, "I can figure this out step by step.")

4. **Program the New Script**—For two weeks, repeat your antidotes every time the old statement appears, even if you don't fully believe them yet.

5. **Watch for the Shift**—Pay attention to your decisions, mood, and energy. Your brain will start following the new blueprint.

Chapter 8
When Words Whisper, the Body Shouts

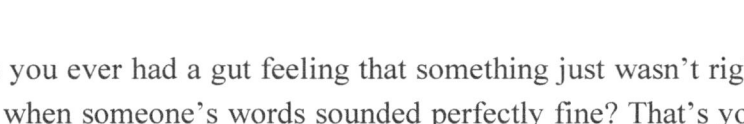

Have you ever had a gut feeling that something just wasn't right, even when someone's words sounded perfectly fine? That's your subconscious picking up on the dissonance between verbal language and body language. While enhancing inner and outer language is vitally important to personal growth, there is another critical component of internal and external interaction that magnifies your self-mastery success.

Body language is the loudest channel in any conversation, broadcasting intent, confidence, and emotion long before words arrive. When you learn to read posture, micro-expressions, gaze, rhythm, space, etc., you see what's *really* being said. For self-mastery, this skill is pivotal because it sharpens situational awareness, reveals your own unconscious signals, and lets you calibrate presence on purpose. You influence more ethically and effectively, protect your boundaries faster, and align your inner state with an outer signal that commands respect, without saying a word.

Most people focus so much on what others are saying that they miss what's being communicated. In negotiations, relationships, or even casual conversation, the body tells the truth more often than the mouth does. Words are easily manipulated. Body language is harder to control, especially under stress, deception, or emotional intensity. Treat this chapter as your entry ramp. The real terrain is wide and technical, so on page 175, I've listed some of the best books I know of in this space. Read them, train with them, and make their methods part of how you speak with and without words.

When a person's body language and spoken message don't align, trust the body. Psychologist Albert Mehrabian famously proposed that:

- 7% of meaning is communicated through spoken words

- 38% through tone of voice

- 55% through body language

While these figures may not be universally applicable, they reinforce a crucial truth: What people do often says more than what they say. You need to be able to identify powerful non-verbal clues to help you detect a mismatch between someone's words and their true feelings. Whether you're a leader, salesperson, coach, or someone who just wants to build deeper connections, these simple hacks will enhance your observational power and presence. For example, if someone says, "I'm fine," but their shoulders are slumped, their voice flat, and they're avoiding eye contact, guess what, they're probably not fine!

In every conversation, whether it's a boardroom pitch, a heartfelt apology, or a first date, there's a second conversation happening just beneath the surface. One that isn't spoken with words, but with posture, tone, expression, and instinct. That second conversation is body language, and it always tells the truth, even when the speaker doesn't. Most people only listen with their ears.

The masters, leaders, negotiators, influencers, and truth-seekers listen with their eyes. That's the edge body language gives you.

It's not just about detecting deception; it's about perceiving intention, reading the room, and recognizing misalignment between what someone says and what they feel. You cannot rely solely on what people say. Words are easy to manipulate. They can be rehearsed, masked, or tailored for approval. But the body? It leaks the truth if you know where to look.

Take, for instance, the forced or asymmetrical smile, one side of the mouth curling up while the eyes stay dead and disengaged. It looks like a smile, but it feels like a lie. Or someone who shakes their head "no" while saying "yes", their body is in protest, even if their mouth isn't. These contradictions matter. They signal dissonance, a red flag that what's being said and what's being felt don't match. Similarly, a person might fidget, cross their arms, or shift uncomfortably while claiming confidence. These leakage gestures, such as touching the face, stepping back while agreeing, and covering the mouth, are signals from the subconscious, revealing nervousness, resistance, or even deceit.

When Things Feel "Off" They Usually Are

Your instincts are ancient and wise. If someone's body language doesn't match their words, you'll feel it. You might not be able to explain why something feels wrong, but your brain is registering the contradiction.

Pay attention to sudden posture shifts, excessive blinking, looking away during direct questions, a sudden change in tone or vocabulary. These aren't "proof" of deception, but they are invitations to dig deeper. Reading body language isn't a party trick, but it's a discipline, and like any skill, it takes training. The goal is to make observation second nature so you don't just analyze behavior, you feel it.

Words Can Betray, but Body Language Can Break Trust

When someone says one thing but acts another, it creates what psychologists call *cognitive dissonance*. The listener is left with a choice to believe the words or believe the signals. If those signals continue to clash, people start believing neither. That's how trust erodes. This disconnect doesn't always mean the person is lying, as it could be fear, stress, or insecurity. But the impact is the same as others begin to doubt.

It Exposes Manipulation or Weak Character

When someone consistently acts out of alignment with their words, it often signals that they're trying to manipulate perception. They lack integrity and may not have the courage to be honest. Even subtle forms of incongruence signal weakness in character, eroding respect and trust.

When someone's actions don't reflect their promises or statements, people begin to guard themselves, stop sharing openly and stop giving the benefit of the doubt. They look for backup plans and distance themselves emotionally. In short, they stop trusting.

Reading body language isn't about accusing or catching people in lies. It's about listening with your eyes and instincts, detecting subtle emotional undercurrents, and choosing your responses with precision.

When you can hear the words and the silence beneath them, you become an elite communicator, someone who sees what others miss and connects on a level that goes far beyond the surface. Words can deceive, but the body always speaks truthfully. Listen with your eyes.

To be trusted, a person must be consistent. That doesn't mean perfect, but it means honest and predictable. Words and actions are congruent. Every time your actions back up your words, you deposit into the "trust bank." Every time they don't, you make a withdrawal and eventually, people close the account.

Body language is a deeply human skill, but there is documented, proven science to it. That's why you must study, experience it, and master it yourself. Observe people. Read books. Pay attention to your own signals. Learn not just to see, but to feel when something is off. Those who can read the silent language of truth are the ones who lead, influence, protect and connect on higher levels. This is more than a skill; it's a superpower. Research it. Learn it. Practice it.

In 1998, the world watched as President Bill Clinton appeared on national television and, with a stern face, said the famous words: "I did not have sexual relations with that woman, Miss Lewinsky." His voice was emphatic. His words were direct. But for many who watched, something didn't feel right. Body language experts and millions of viewers noticed:

- *His jaw clenched and his lips pressed tightly together, a classic sign of tension and withholding.*

- *He shook his head slightly, "no," even as he forcefully said "yes" to his own denial.*

- *His gaze was unusually fixed, not connecting naturally with the camera, which made his words feel rehearsed rather than authentic.*

There were brief flashes of anger and defensiveness in his micro-expressions—signals that often leak out when a person is under pressure or hiding something. In the following months, as the scandal unfolded, it became clear that Clinton had not told the truth. People who had doubted his words cited not just the facts, but how he looked and sounded in that moment. His verbal denial was powerful, but his body language planted a seed of suspicion that his words alone could not erase. The truth was eventually exposed—not by what he said, but by what he showed. This high-profile moment is a textbook example of the principle: When words and body disagree, trust the body. Millions of people sensed something was "off," even before evidence came out. They couldn't always explain it, but their intuition picked up on the mismatch—proving how deeply wired we are to detect incongruence. Trust is built on congruence, the alignment of words, tone, and body. When they diverge, even slightly, people feel it. Leaders, negotiators, and everyday people are judged not by their speech alone, but by their presence. When body language betrays the spoken message, credibility crumbles. You don't have to be a trained expert to sense the truth. Your instincts—honed over millennia—are constantly scanning for signs of honesty or deception.

Tactical Tool: The Silent Second Conversation Method

Over the years, I've interviewed hundreds of people seeking sales positions with our companies. Early in the conversation, I ask a throwaway-sounding question: "Do you enjoy cold calling?" I don't actually care too much about the word that comes out next, but I do care whether their words and body language match. When I hear "yes" while the head subtly shakes "no," that's a red flag. From that point on, I ran the rest of the interview with that mismatch in mind and on the lookout for more. The mouth speaks a language the body can't always mirror. Next time you talk to someone, treat their words as a "caption" and their body language as a "movie." Watch the movie more than the caption. Notice the posture, the expressions, the shifts in tone. Let your instincts weigh in. Often, the feeling you get before you have "evidence" is the most accurate signal you'll ever receive. Five questions to anchor the lesson:

1. What is one recent conversation where the body language told me something the words did not?

2. In what types of situations am I most likely to ignore my gut when it senses a mismatch?

3. How can I train myself to spot "baseline changes" in people I interact with regularly?

4. What habits or signals in my own body language could be undermining my credibility?

5. How might consistently trusting and acting on these observations change the way I lead, negotiate, or connect?

Chapter 9
The Kingdom of This Moment

"How strange is man. He destroys his present while worrying about his future, but weeps in his future, worrying about his past."

—Imam Ali

Our minds tend to drift between what might happen and what has already happened, leaving the present, the only place where life occurs, neglected and unlived. While we are aware enough to know we're temporary, we're not equipped to live every second as if we truly understood what that means.

The present moment is the only space where we can act, feel, connect, heal, and grow. Yet we squander it, trading it for anxieties about the future or guilt from the past, neither of which we can control.

The tragedy is that the future we worry about never arrives as expected, and the past we mourn is already set in stone. If we could learn to root ourselves in the now, breathing it in, noticing its texture, and be grateful for its gift, we'd find a well of peace and clarity that doesn't exist anywhere else.

The present is where joy resides, love expresses itself and where purpose takes shape. There is a quiet, enduring strength that comes from mastering the art of living in the present moment. Philosophers, coaches, and spiritual guides have returned to the same essential truth: live life in the now. Marcus Aurelius reminded himself daily that the past is beyond our reach, the future uncertain, and that the present is our only true possession. Similarly, Viktor Frankl wrote that even in the direst circumstances, the ability to find meaning in the moment at hand is what preserves one's humanity.

Yet so many of us replay conversations, relive failures, and rehearse disasters that may never come. Ecclesiastes reflects on the fleeting nature of all things under the sun, teaching that the endless chase for meaning in the uncontrollable leads only to frustration. In the same spirit, John Wooden, the legendary coach, insisted that we focus not on outcomes, but on effort in the present. Why is staying present so difficult? Our minds are wired for survival and depend on remembering mistakes and anticipating dangers. Because we are not being chased by saber-toothed predators, this wiring often works against us. We trade peace for rumination. Eckhart Tolle, in his work *The Power of Now*, describes how identifying too strongly with our thoughts and fears pulls us away from the now.

Beating yourself up over the past is one of the most common ways we lose the present. This is a form of mental self-violence that serves no one. The Stoics taught that what has happened is no longer in our control; it exists only in memory, and memory is unreliable. Seneca noted, "We suffer more in imagination than in reality." The past can only be useful as a teacher, not as a judge. When you find yourself stuck on a past failure, ask yourself, "What actionable lesson can I take from this?" If there is one, note it. Then, let the rest go as you would release a bird from a cage. Worrying about the future is the other thief of presence. Planning is wise, but worrying is not. Planning involves concrete steps based on present information. Worrying is often unstructured fear that drains rather than builds. Viktor Frankl survived by focusing on small moments of control, such as his thoughts or a kind word to a fellow prisoner. If we can center ourselves in the now, we can retain agency.

Most people live as prisoners of psychological time, endlessly reliving the past or anxiously anticipating the future. When you come to live fully in the present, these emotions change shape with some dissolving and others evolving. The key to this transformation is certainly logical yet requires tremendous commitment, discipline and practice to be here, now.

Fear Lives in the Future

As discussed in Chapter 5, fear is almost always about what might happen. It is your imagination running simulations of failure, pain, or loss, all in a time that hasn't even arrived. Whether it's fear of being rejected, failing, aging, losing control, or dying, it's all rooted in the belief that something in the future will be unbearable. But in the present, fear cannot survive.

In this exact moment, this breath, this heartbeat, you are simply alive. When you step into the present moment, fear becomes a whisper rather than a scream, and you should realize most of what you fear is just a thought, and thoughts are not threats. "The psychological condition of fear is divorced from any concrete and true immediate danger. It comes in many forms; unease, worry, anxiety, nervousness, tension, dread, and phobia. This kind of fear is always of something that might happen, not of something that is happening now." —Eckhart Tolle.

When you truly enter the present, the space between stimulus and reaction opens wide, and in that space, courage emerges.

Guilt Lives in the Past

Guilt is a byproduct of memory by clinging to what was, what you did or didn't do, said or didn't say. It's often wrapped in shame and colored by judgment. But the past does not exist as anything real, only as a thought. Thoughts about the past are filtered through today's mind, emotions, and perceptions. They are often distorted, amplified, or weaponized against your own peace. The miracle of presence is that it invites forgiveness not just of others, but of yourself. In the present, you remember that you were unconscious when you made mistakes. You were acting from fear, pain, or ego, just as everyone else does when they hurt someone. Presence is not passive. It allows you to take responsibility without making mistakes. It sees what happened, but it doesn't relive it. When you anchor into the now, guilt has nowhere to stick. Because you are no longer identifying with who you were, you are here now and aware.

Even Optimism Can Be a Trap

Optimism is often celebrated as a virtue, and it can be. But when optimism is tied to future outcomes ("I'll be happy when . . ." or "It will all work out someday . . ."), it becomes a form of subtle denial. You postpone peace and escape into hope. Hope isn't always helpful if it pulls you away from what is. Presence, instead, gives rise to true power and a grounded form of joy that doesn't depend on conditions. From presence comes not blind optimism, but conscious creation. It's the difference between hoping life will change and realizing you can respond powerfully to what life is offering you now.

"What a liberation to realize that the 'voice in my head' is not who I am. Who am I then? The one who sees that." —Eckhart Tolle. When you are fully present, you don't need to hope for a better moment, as this one is enough. From that fullness, action arises not from lack, but from stillness and clarity. Identifying when you've fallen out of the present is a skill. Signs to notice are racing thoughts, tension in the body, or feeling lost in thought while missing what's directly before you. Others may experience irritability or sudden sadness that feels disproportionate to the moment.

When this happens, pause, and check in with your body; are your shoulders tight, is your jaw clenched, or are you taking short breaths? Simply becoming aware is often enough to bring you back. Recovery from being lost in the past or future involves intentional re-centering. Here are a few practical techniques:

- **To clear your mind instantly**: Ask yourself, "What is my next thought?"

- **Anchor to the Senses:** Focus on what you can see, hear, touch, taste, and smell right now. The Stoics often recommended reminding themselves of the raw facts of their immediate reality.

- **Breath Awareness:** As Eckhart Tolle emphasizes, the breath is always present. Five deep, slow breaths can quiet the mind.

- **Single-Tasking:** Choose to do one thing and do it fully. Whether it is washing dishes or writing a letter, immerse yourself in the task.

- **Gratitude Lists:** Writing down three things you are grateful for, right now, can shift attention from fear or regret to appreciation.

- **Reframing Thoughts:** Ask yourself, "Is this thought about the past or future helping me right now?" If not, release it.

- **Observe your thoughts without judgment:** You are not your thoughts; you are the awareness behind them.

- **Feel your body:** Notice the aliveness in your hands, your feet, your chest. Presence always begins in the body.

- **Accept this moment fully:** Even if it's unpleasant, even if it hurts. Resistance feeds fear and guilt. Acceptance dissolves them.

Living in the present moment does not mean abandoning responsibility or becoming indifferent to consequences. It means accepting that action and peace both live in the now. Ultimately, staying present is about practicing awareness, discipline, and grace toward yourself. You will fall out of the moment as we all do. What matters is how quickly and gently you bring yourself back. This is the quiet mastery at the heart of self-leadership. To live well is to live now.

Interactive Exercise—Present Moment Reconnection Practice

Every evening for the next seven days, complete the following journal prompts:

One moment today when I caught myself worrying about the future or regretting the past:

How I noticed it:

What I did to return to the present:

How I felt afterward:

By making this a regular practice, you strengthen your presence.

Building Awareness of Your Mental Patterns

When you pause each evening to reflect on a moment you drifted into worry or regret, you're engaging the observer within you. You're training yourself to notice your thoughts rather than be consumed by them. This separation, between you and your thinking, is the foundation of emotional intelligence and self-mastery.

Practice Returning to the Present Moment

By recording what brought you back to the now—your breath, a grounding technique, a shift in focus - you strengthen that mental muscle. Each time you do it, it becomes easier to return home to yourself. Instead of berating yourself for drifting mentally, this practice invites gentle redirection. You can now learn to guide your mind like a wise parent would guide a child. Over the seven days, you'll begin to see patterns.

At certain times of day might trigger worry, or you may be more prone to regret after social interactions. That type of insight is gold, and with it, you shift from unconscious reaction to conscious response and become the architect of your inner world. That's the essence of self-mastery...learning to lead your mind instead of being led by it. Do it for seven days. Watch what happens. The quiet clarity you'll cultivate might just surprise you.

Freedom Through Presence

Fear, guilt, and false optimism are not flaws of character. They are symptoms of being lost in time. When you return to the present, not just mentally but in your entire being, these emotional ghosts begin to fade. You see clearly. You act with intention. You love without grasping. And most importantly, you *live*. In a world constantly pulling you into the past and the future, the ability to stay present is a superpower. As Eckhart Tolle reminds us: "Wherever you are, be there totally. If you find your here, and now intolerable . . . leave it. If you can't leave it, accept it. All else is madness." Keep these reminders where you'll see them often. Post them on your desk, set them as a phone wallpaper, or write them on your bathroom mirror. Let these ancient and modern voices guide you back whenever your mind wanders. Let the madness go. Come back. The present is waiting.

After her divorce, Lisa found herself caught in a loop of regret and anxiety. She replayed every mistake she believed she made in her marriage, what she said, what she didn't say, the decisions she'd change if given the chance. She also lived with a persistent fear about the future: Would she ever find love again? Would her children be okay? Would she end up alone? These thoughts filled her days and kept her up at night. Because her mind was always pulled backward or forward, Lisa struggled to enjoy anything in the present. Even during pleasant moments like dinner with friends, reading with her kids, or a walk in the park, her mind wandered. She felt distracted, tense, and unable to relax. Over time, this chronic state of regret and worry led to exhaustion, irritability, and even health issues. The richness of her life in the little joys, the peace of a quiet morning, and the warmth of genuine connection were dulled by mental noise. It wasn't until Lisa learned about and started practicing mindfulness that she realized how much her mind's fixation on the past and future had cost her. As she slowly learned to let go, forgive herself, and focus on the present moment, she began to feel lighter and more at peace. She found that contentment wasn't waiting for her in some distant future or lost in the past, but was available right now, in the simple act of truly being present. This is the silent toll of living outside the present: It steals our ability to experience clarity, connection, and contentment, even when life itself is offering them to us.

Tactical Tool: The Present Moment Rescue Protocol

While on a long cross-country flight, I was having a conversation with a man who had lost nearly everything. His business, his marriage, and his health were all falling apart. As we spoke, he was clearly distraught, and mentioned several times that he kept asking himself, *"What I should have done differently."* Then after a long pause, *". . . and what might go wrong next."* His conversation with himself reveals what steals so many lives, and that's living everywhere but here. The irony was that, in the chair next to me, in that moment, he was safe. He was fed. He was breathing. He wasn't being attacked or humiliated. But his mind was. We all fight ghosts from the past or shadowbox with futures that don't exist.

The skill is to notice when you've drifted and return. Here's how to start: The next time you catch yourself replaying a regret or rehearsing a fear, stop. Feel your feet on the ground. Take one slow, deliberate breath in and out. Then ask, "What's actually happening right now?" You'll realize that in this exact moment, almost nothing is wrong. The danger is in the thought, not the now. And if something *is* wrong, your power to act is here, not in memory or imagination. Five Questions to Anchor the Lesson:

1. What's one specific way I lose the present to regrets about the past?

2. What's one specific way I lose the present to fears about the future?

3. When I am fully here and now, what sensations do I notice in my body?

4. How might my decision-making change if I always acted from the present instead of from fear or guilt?

5. What's one small ritual I can use daily to bring myself back to the now?

Chapter 10
Chosen Companions, Chosen Destiny

"The key is to keep company only with people who uplift you, whose presence calls forth your best."

—Epictetus

The Stoics believed that your character is shaped not just by what you do alone, but by what you absorb from the people around you. Every conversation, shared emotion and every influence seeps into your thoughts, ultimately driving your actions. What people do once is chance, but what they do repeatedly is who they are. Stay close only to the right ones. If you spend time with people who gossip, complain, or envy, you eventually echo those traits. But if you're surrounded by those who are courageous, honest, disciplined and kind, you rise to meet their level.

Why Toxic People Hold You Back

Toxic individuals often operate from fear, insecurity, and scarcity. They may belittle your ambition, undermine your confidence, or even secretly root for your failure, while not always out of malice, but your growth can highlight their stagnation. Keeping them close isn't just unwise, but dangerous to your mindset. Just as weeds choke out healthy plants in a garden, toxic people crowd out your potential, making it harder for your goals to flourish. King Solomon, in all his wisdom, understood this. He wrote, "Walk with the wise and become wise, for a companion of fools suffers harm."

– Proverbs 13:20. This verse also echoes the Stoic principle that we are shaped by proximity. Wisdom and success are not isolated achievements and are fostered in wise company. The fool's presence is contagious, and you must be aware of the destructive power of poor associations and how critical it is to guard your inner circle.

The Power of a Positive Environment

A nourishing environment acts as sunlight and water to the soul. When you are surrounded by people who celebrate your growth, challenge your excuses, and remind you of your potential, you naturally rise. You begin to believe in your own abilities because those around you reinforce that belief with their words and example.

Viktor Frankl emphasized the power of meaning and inner strength in even the darkest conditions, but he also made clear that human beings can and do help one another endure, evolve and thrive. In the camps, those who held onto hope, who encouraged others, who gave their last piece of bread, created a culture of survival and dignity, even in the midst of horror. Imagine how powerful that is in your own life when you're not surviving but striving. A supportive, high-character community is fuel for your best self.

You Rise or Fall with Your Circle

Ultimately, who you surround yourself with determines the emotional climate you live in. If that climate is polluted by envy, negativity and fear, your goals suffocate. But if it's filled with encouragement and accountability, our growth accelerates. The Stoics, King Solomon, and Frankl each offer different roads to the same destination of truth, virtue, and flourishing, and none of them suggests you can get there alone. I've seen it time and again; if you spend time with five confident people, their mindset becomes contagious. You'll start walking taller, thinking bigger, and speaking with purpose. If you surround yourself with five people who prioritize health, discipline, and energy, you'll naturally rise to that standard. Hanging around intelligence and curiosity becomes your habit. But the opposite is equally true because if you linger too long with toxic, negative, or complacent people, you'll absorb their limitations like secondhand smoke.

Your circle is your ecosystem, and it will either nurture your growth or poison your progress. So be intentional and audit your circle like your life depends on it, because in many ways it does. Choose people who elevate you, not tolerate you, and you won't just survive, you'll thrive. If someone dims your light, it's not noble to let them stay. It's not compassionate to shrink for their comfort, as it is a disservice to your purpose. Choose the atmosphere in which your soul can breathe, as that's where you'll flourish. Life isn't just made of victories; it's made of valleys, poor decisions, failed plans, unexpected illness, and emotional collapse.

In those moments, your environment must offer grace, not shame. Growth requires truth without condemnation. The Stoics taught that external events are neither good nor bad, but it is our judgment of them that creates suffering. When you're surrounded by those who don't judge you, you are given space to reflect without the added burden of shame. They remind you that you're not only your worst day, but a soul in progress. King Solomon, in all his divine wisdom, wrote, "A friend loves at all times, and a brother is born for adversity." — Proverbs 17:17

Those who stand beside you when you're weak, without judgment or without turning away, are rare and necessary. They reflect God's mercy and offer you a safe place to process, heal, and evolve. Judgment shuts people down and breeds secrecy, fear, and self-loathing. But nonjudgmental presence creates a container where honesty can live. Only then can we take full responsibility for our mistakes, not to wallow in guilt, but to learn and rise from them. You can't change what you pretend isn't there. And you won't be honest about what you fear being judged for.

People who accept you without judgment aren't just being kind; they're acting as mirrors of grace and strength. They help you see yourself clearly when your vision is clouded by pain or regret. Their acceptance becomes your foundation, and from that place of inner security, you can make better decisions, heal faster, and become wiser. Include people who don't judge you, especially when you're at your worst, because they make room for your humanity, not just your perfection. They allow you to fall forward, and remind you that mistakes are lessons, not life sentences, with people who won't hold you hostage to your past because you don't have to stay there.

Identifying Toxic People and Knowing How to Handle Them

This is essential for protecting your mental clarity, emotional energy, and life trajectory. Toxic individuals are often subtle in their influence at first, but over time, they can drain your self-worth, block your progress, and keep you stuck in cycles of guilt, self-doubt, or even fear. Here's how to identify them and handle them wisely:

- **They constantly criticize or belittle you:** It's masked as "jokes," "just being honest," or "trying to help," but it always leaves you feeling smaller. Their words rarely build, but tear down.

- **They drain your energy:** After spending time with them, you feel emotionally exhausted instead of uplifted. You may feel anxious, resentful, or less motivated.

- **They play the victim or manipulate emotions:** They twist situations so they're always the one hurt or wronged, making you feel guilty, even when you've done nothing wrong.

- **They're threatened by your growth:** When you succeed or improve, they respond with sarcasm, silence, or subtle sabotage. They don't celebrate you, but they compete with you, many times through lies and attempted manipulation.

- **They don't respect boundaries:** They ignore your limits, pressure you to do things you don't want to do, or make you feel guilty for saying "no."

How to Handle Toxic People

- **Don't be surprised that people can act a particular way:** Stoics believe that people will sometimes act harshly or disappoint you, not out of personal spite, but because that's human nature…like being in a boxing match. Would you be surprised if your opponent tried to punch you? Understanding this is like knowing the fight will be tough, you show up ready, not surprised or bitter, but steady and resilient. "When you wake up in the morning, remind yourself that some of the people you deal with today will be meddling, ungrateful, arrogant, dishonest, jealous, and surly." – Marcus Aurelius

- **Get clear on your values:** Like the Stoics taught, know who you are. Once you're anchored in your values (peace, discipline, growth, kindness.), it becomes easier to spot when someone is misaligned with them.

- **Set strong boundaries without guilt:** Toxic people feed off blurred lines. You don't need to explain or argue. A firm, respectful "I won't engage in this," or "That doesn't work for me," is enough. Protecting your peace is not rude, it's wise.

- **Limit access:** Not everyone deserves front-row seats to your life. You can love someone from a distance or reduce interaction gradually. You're not obligated to keep people in your circle just because of history.

- **Don't take the bait:** Stay calm and stoic in the face of provocation. As Marcus Aurelius said: "The best revenge is to be unlike him who performed the injury." Rise above and don't mirror their dysfunction.

- **Choose a better company:** King Solomon said, "Iron sharpens iron, so one man sharpens another." Seek people who sharpen you, not those who dull your spirit. Friends who speak life into you are not optional; they're your oxygen.

- **Detach emotionally when needed:** You may not be able to change a person, but you can always change your reaction, your exposure, and your investment in them.

Final Thought on Toxic People in Your Life

You don't have to hate toxic people, but you do have to stop letting them shape your reality. Your peace, potential, and purpose are too valuable to be held hostage by insecurity, envy, or manipulation. Don't worry about criticism from people you wouldn't take advice from, because they, whether accidentally or on purpose, limit your potential to grow. Let go of those who hold you back and create space for those who call you higher. That's where your true growth begins and is part of how the profoundness of your life is determined.

Identifying Good Strong People

Identifying strong, good people to support your growth, as well as knowing how to identify, handle and nurture those relationships, is extremely valuable to you. These people are the ones who fuel your momentum, challenge your excuses, and celebrate your success without insecurity. Here's how to spot them and build strong relationships:

- **They live what they speak:** Look for people whose actions align with their words and values. They show integrity in private and public. As the Stoics said, "Don't listen to what a man says, but watch what he does."

- **They hold themselves accountable:** Strong people take ownership of their choices. They don't blame, deflect, play victim or make excuses. They grow through adversity and inspire others to do the same.

- **They challenge you with love:** These people won't just hype you up, but will correct you when needed, with kindness and without judgment. They push you toward your potential, not their ego.

- **They're not threatened by your success:** Instead of competing, they cheer for you genuinely. Their self-worth is rooted in growth, not comparison. They understand that another's success doesn't diminish their own, but in fact, it enhances it.

- **They're consistent**: You can trust their character over time, not always perfect, but steady, grounded, and present. They don't vanish when life gets hard, and they don't gossip when you're not in the room.

Nurturing Those Relationships

- **Reciprocate the energy:** Good people deserve your best. If they support you, support them. Show up, speak truth, and invest time. Water the relationship. Strong people don't stick around when they feel one-sided loyalty.

- **Be open to correction:** Let them challenge you without defensiveness. As Proverbs says: "Wounds from a friend can be trusted, but an enemy multiplies kisses." Truth from someone who loves you is a gift, not an insult.

- **Create space for honesty:** Invite real conversations. Authentically say things like: "I trust your judgment, and if I'm missing something, call me on it." That vulnerability deepens the connection and helps you grow faster.

- **Respect their boundaries and values:** Just because they're strong doesn't mean they don't need space, rest, or their own dreams. Support their growth, too. Strong people need and generally attract strong friends.

- **Show gratitude often:** Don't wait to say thank you. Express appreciation in words and actions. A message, a favor, a moment of acknowledgment go a long way. Even the strongest people need encouragement.

Good people are rare, and when you find them, don't treat them casually. Grow with them and become one of them. Sit at tables where they're plotting your success. Together, you'll go farther than you ever could alone.

LeBron James didn't just become an NBA legend because of raw talent. He surrounded himself from an early age with people who genuinely wanted to see him succeed and who challenged him to grow. As a teenager growing up in Akron, Ohio, LeBron faced constant instability, poverty, and an absent father, moving from apartment ·to apartment. What made the difference? He built a tight circle with a handful of friends—Maverick Carter, Rich Paul, and Randy Mims—who believed in something bigger than basketball. These friends weren't yes-men. They called him out when he drifted, reminded him of his purpose, and kept him grounded. As his fame skyrocketed, LeBron didn't replace them with people who only wanted something from him. Instead, he invested in these relationships and helped empower his friends to become business partners, trusted advisors, and voices of accountability. This inner circle challenged each other, celebrated wins, and offered tough love in private when needed. Their collective ambition and loyalty became a fortress against the usual trappings of stardom, like scandals, poor financial choices, or ego-driven mistakes. LeBron has openly said that his friends "saved him from himself" more than once, pushing him to make decisions aligned with his values and vision, not just his talent.

Tactical Tool: The Circle Audit Ritual

Some people are like sunlight, and they pull you toward growth. Others are like slow poison, as you won't feel it at first, but it will hollow you out. Treat your inner circle like a vault. Only the purest gold gets in. Everything else stays out. Audit your circle with the precision of a jeweler inspecting diamonds. If they don't shine, they don't stay. Answer the following without guilt to protect your mind, magnify your growth, and curate your inner circle with intention:

1. Who in my life consistently makes me feel lighter, stronger, and more alive after I'm with them?

2. Who subtly drains my energy, sows doubt, or pulls my focus from my purpose?

3. Which relationship needs clearer boundaries? What's one step I can take to set them?

4. Who embodies the values I want to grow into, and how can I spend more time with them?

5. If my future depended on my current circle, would I be confident or concerned?

Chapter 11
Get Comfortable Being Uncomfortable

"The magic you are looking for is in the work you are avoiding."
—Dipen Parmar

This deceptively simple statement hits hard, especially when viewed through the lens of psychology, philosophy, and personal growth. Avoidance is a subtle form of surrender. When we dodge difficult conversations, actions, uncomfortable emotions, past traumas or challenging decisions, we are not freeing ourselves but binding ourselves to them. The more you try to suppress or escape fear, truth or responsibility, the more power it gains over your thoughts, behavior, and ultimately your freedom. Evasion can show up as procrastination, anxiety, addiction, perfectionism or emotional detachment.

The hardest battle you have to fight is between your old habits and your new standards. Poor habits are typically designed to be a protective shield, and they keep us small, reactive and disconnected from our potential. Carl Jung said, "What you resist, persists." And Viktor Frankl taught that meaning can only be found in facing our suffering, not in fleeing it.

The Stoics, too, were adamant that you don't run from discomfort, but lean into it, prepare for it and even welcome it. What you avoid becomes your master, and fortunately, what you confront becomes your servant. A few examples:

- Avoiding conflict allows resentment to build and erodes relationships.

- Avoiding failure stops you from ever taking the risks needed to grow.

- Avoiding grief delays healing and keeps you emotionally stuck.

- Avoiding the truth about your habits, your health, or your choices silently sabotages your future.

The Remedy

- Whatever scares you, walk toward it with awareness.

- Whatever you've been putting off, tackle it head-on.

- Whatever you've buried, dig it up, look it in the eye, and strip it of its power.

- Mastery, peace, and growth begin the moment you stop running.

Most often, when you choose to dodge tough things, you can take on a victim mentality, and that is the silent killer of personal growth and self-mastery. When you see yourself as a victim, you hand over the keys to your own power. You begin to believe that your circumstances, your past, or other people are in control of your future.

The truth is that you can't confront what you're avoiding if you've convinced yourself it's someone else's responsibility. Avoidance thrives in the soil of self-pity and gives you permission to stay stuck, make excuses, and delay the hard, uncomfortable, but necessary inner work. Growth demands ownership. You have to say, "This may not be my fault, but it is my fight." The moment you shift from "Why me?" to "What now?" you reclaim the ability to self-master. The victim mindset keeps you looping through the same patterns, afraid to face pain, afraid to fail, afraid to heal. Remember that self-mastery is paved in responsibility, accountability and discipline.

The moment you stop pointing outward and start looking inward, your outlook goes up. You are not powerless or broken, but you must choose to rise. There's a stark difference between being affected by circumstances and being defined by them. Everyone faces setbacks, loss, betrayals, unfairness, illness and failures, but not everyone allows those things to dictate who they become. When you live in a victim mindset, you say:

- I can't because of them.

- I'm stuck because of this.

- I would, but life isn't fair.

To many, that mindset may feel safe, but it's a cage dressed in velvet. It gives you an excuse not to try, not to grow, not to take responsibility because if it's always them, it never has to be you. History, philosophy and experience have clearly proven that greatness is often born from adversity.

- Nelson Mandela spent 27 years in prison and came out as a leader of unity.

- Viktor Frankl lost everything in the Holocaust and taught the world about finding meaning in suffering.

- Helen Keller was deaf and blind and became a symbol of resilience and intelligence.

What separated them wasn't that their circumstances were easy. They refused to let those circumstances own their identity. You regain control when you rise above the victim role. Responsibility is not blame, but ownership of your life, no matter what cards you were dealt.

Growth requires discomfort, risk and ownership. Victimhood avoids all three. You become magnetic. People gravitate toward those who face life with courage and resilience, not those who stay stuck in the story of "why me." You write your own story. When you stop seeing yourself as a victim, you become the author, not just a character.

Ask yourself:

- Do I want to be pitied or strong?

- Do I want to just survive or grow to my potential?

- Do I want to live in the story of my pain or the story of my purpose?

Your circumstances may be your starting point, not your final chapter. As Marcus Aurelius said, "The impediment to action advances action, what stands in the way becomes the way." Stop waiting for the world to change. Change within, and the world begins to follow.

Before founding Spanx, Sara Blakely was a door-to-door fax machine salesperson, hardly the glamorous launchpad for a future billionaire. For years, she dreamed of starting her own business, but the fear of failure and embarrassment held her back. She avoided working on her idea, telling herself she didn't have enough money, experience, or credibility. The thought of rejection from investors and manufacturers was overwhelming, so she procrastinated, keeping her dream on the back burner. But Blakely's breakthrough came the moment she stopped running from the hard, uncomfortable work. She forced herself to confront every obstacle head-on: she wrote her own patent (because she couldn't afford a lawyer), cold-called factories until one finally agreed to work with her and pitched her product to skeptical retailers in person.

Every step required her to face rejection, fear, and self-doubt, the exact things she had been avoiding for years. Instead of letting the discomfort stop her, Blakely learned to see it as a signal: "The magic you're looking for is in the work you're avoiding." That mindset shift turned her biggest weaknesses, which were her lack of connections, funding, and industry knowledge, into her greatest strengths. She built Spanx from scratch, became the world's youngest self-made female billionaire, and credits her success not to luck, but to finally doing the hard, scary work she'd been dodging. Your next level lives on the other side of discomfort. Blakely's story is a living example that the breakthroughs we seek, whether in business or life, come not from sidestepping fear, but by walking right through it. What you avoid isn't your barrier; it's your gateway.

Tactical Tool: The Avoidance-to-Action Protocol

In 1989, fresh out of college, I took a job selling long-distance telephone services to small to medium-sized businesses. No leads, no appointments, unless I set them, just forty face-to-face cold knocks a day in office towers, five days a week, eight + hours a day. My job was to convince the receptionist to pull the decision-maker from their office to the lobby, then quickly convince the decision-maker to walk back to their office with me, then let me do my sales pitch and close the deal using the "Seven Steps to a Sale" process.

At first, it was terrifying. I was young, green, and although I had been given great sales training, I had no clue what I was doing. But day after day, I got sharper. I learned to read people in seconds, to handle rejections without flinching, and to turn strangers into customers on the spot. That grind didn't just build my career, it built me. It taught me lessons about people, persistence, and leadership that still shape my life today. If I'd dodged that job because it was hard, I'd have missed the very thing that made so much else possible. Contemplate the following:

1. What's the single task, truth, or decision I've been dodging the longest?

2. If I faced it today, what's the worst realistic outcome and could I survive it?

3. What's the cost of continuing to avoid it over the next year?

4. Who could stand beside me or hold me accountable as I take the first step?

5. How will my life expand once this weight is gone?

Chapter 12
Discipline is the Scaffolding of Dreams

"Discipline is doing something you hate
but doing it like you love it."

—Mike Tyson

Discipline is not punishment. It is protection and the invisible architecture that supports the quiet force behind every life of purpose, peace, self-mastery and power. Without it, as King Solomon warned, your life becomes defenseless, like a city exposed to the chaos of impulses, distractions and poor choices.

Musonius Rufus, the Roman Stoic philosopher and teacher of Epictetus, wrote: "Discipline is a kind of training which makes the soul accustomed to enduring hard things." That daily training leads to governing your own mind, rather than being ruled by circumstance or emotion. It is the art of doing what is right over what is easy, and what is meaningful over what is momentarily satisfying.

Discipline is not about rigidity, but alignment. When your actions match your words, values, goals, and your higher calling, that is discipline. It's waking up early, not because you must, but because your mission matters more than your comfort. It's saying no to temptations because you're devoted to something bigger and better.

King Solomon said in Proverbs 13:11, "Wealth gained hastily will dwindle, but whoever gathers little by little will increase it." Discipline is the gathering of small victories and those quiet habits repeated in the dark, leading to a brilliant life in the light. To Stoics, discipline was not optional; it was sacred. People may have dreams, talent, and intelligence, but without discipline, they die in the realm of potential.

Discipline gives structure to ambition, and it builds the bridge between who you are and who you could become. Every great legacy, from ancient kings to modern leaders, was built not just on inspiration but on relentless war against distraction, laziness, and indulgence.

So the question is not, "Do you want self-mastery success?" It is, "Do you want to pay the price for it daily, in small private acts of discipline?" That is the only currency the universe accepts. Not wishes or words, but action, done even when no one's watching. Discipline doesn't restrict your freedom; it creates it. And that's how you move from merely existing to reigning over your life like the philosopher kings before you.

Procrastination is another subtle form of self-betrayal. It whispers lies like, "You'll feel more ready later," "There's still time," or "It's okay to wait." What it really does is slowly erode your confidence, clarity and your character. The Stoics were brutal in their honesty about time. Marcus Aurelius said, "You could leave life right now. Let that determine what you do, say, and think."

Procrastination is the arrogant assumption that life will give you more time, opportunities and chances to be who you were meant to become. But nothing is promised. Every hour delayed is an hour of growth, progress, or impact lost forever. Personal growth requires tension and demands that you stretch beyond what you think you are capable of. You become stuck in a cycle of intentions never acted on, goals never pursued, and dreams that slowly rot into regret. "A little sleep, a little slumber, a little folding of the hands to rest and poverty will come on you like a thief."—Proverbs 6:10-11.

Poverty is not just of money but of soul, discipline and purpose. You can't become wise if you always wait, and you won't grow stronger if you always delay. You can't build anything of lasting value on a foundation of excuses and tomorrow-thinking. Growth requires urgency and presence, not panic.

Procrastination keeps you mentally busy but spiritually stagnant. It tricks you into feeling safe, while your dreams slowly drift out of reach. What you postpone today becomes your burden tomorrow, with every decision delayed becoming a weight added to your future self.

Whatever you're putting off is likely the very thing that will elevate you. That's the signal, as the resistance you feel is the compass pointing toward your next level. So, embrace discipline and put off procrastination or waiting for the perfect moment. That moment is now, maybe bruised, uncertain and unfinished, but it's yours, and in it lies the power to break the cycle and move.

Procrastination is a thief, but unlike most thieves, it doesn't break in. You invite it and let it rob you of the one thing you can never get back…time. So, take the moment, the risk and the step, because while procrastination steals . . . discipline builds. Today is still under your command.

Kobe Bryant, the late NBA legend, was famous not just for his talent but for his almost mythical work ethic and discipline. Early in his career, Kobe wasn't the strongest or the fastest What set him apart was his refusal to be outworked.

While other players celebrated after games or slept in on off days, Kobe was in the gym before sunrise, shooting thousands of free throws, running sprints, perfecting his footwork. He called this relentless commitment "The Mamba Mentality," which was nothing less than a devotion to discipline above all else.

Kobe Bryant's discipline was legendary, and the stories are as inspiring as they are concrete. Here are several vivid examples that show exactly how he built those "walls" of self-control:

1. Early Morning Workouts:

Kobe was notorious for his 4 a.m. workouts. Even during the offseason or before regular practices, he would arrive at the gym in the dead of night—often before anyone else in the organization was awake. There are countless accounts from teammates and trainers who tried to "beat Kobe to the gym," only to find he was already there, drenched in sweat, having already completed hours of shooting drills and conditioning.

2. The 1,000 Shots Rule:

Kobe regularly made himself shoot 1,000 jump shots in a single workout session. He would not allow himself to leave the gym until he hit that number, no matter how tired or sore he was. This relentless repetition wasn't about punishment, it was about mastery, ensuring that when the pressure was highest, his skills would not fail him.

3. Obsession with Details:

Bryant studied the game obsessively, breaking down film not just of his own games, but of legendary players before him like Michael Jordan, Magic Johnson, Larry Bird. He would analyze their footwork, shot selection, and mental approach, then replicate and adapt those techniques in his own training. Kobe's discipline extended to his diet, sleep, and even mental training, often meditating to sharpen his focus.

4. Playing Through Injury:

In 2013, Bryant famously ruptured his Achilles tendon during a critical game. Most athletes would collapse, but Kobe got up, limped to the free-throw line, and made both shots before walking off the court on his own. This moment symbolized his entire career: Pain and adversity were obstacles to overcome, not reasons to quit.

5. The "No Excuses" Mindset:

Kobe's discipline wasn't just about physical preparation. It was about refusing to let excuses, distractions, or comfort get in the way of his mission. During the 2008 Olympics, his Team USA teammates recounted that while they were coming back to the hotel from a night out, Kobe was already headed to the gym for his second workout of the day. He didn't let success breed complacency; he used every day as an opportunity to outwork everyone.

Kobe Bryant's discipline made him a fortress in a world of temptation and distraction. His daily, often unseen choices were the building blocks of his greatness. For Kobe, discipline wasn't a restriction, but a liberation. It allowed him to rise above the chaos of ego, fatigue, and doubt, and to achieve what few ever will. His life and legacy are living proof. Discipline is not punishment; it's protection and the key to unlocking extraordinary potential.

Tactical Tool: The Daily Discipline Fortress Builder

There's a moment, every single day, when you stand at the fork between comfort and commitment. No audience. No applause. Just you, the work, and the choice. This is where discipline is made, not in the fire of inspiration, but in the cold mornings, the late nights, the thousand small refusals to quit. Discipline is not a mood. It's a covenant you make with yourself and keep when no one is watching. It is the steel in your spine when your body says "stop" and your mind says "later." Freedom isn't escape from effort; it's the mastery of it. Five questions to temper your will:

1. If my life were judged only by what I do when I'm alone, what would that verdict be?

2. What is one thing I could finish today, no matter what, that would strengthen my self-respect?

3. How would I act if my legacy depended on what I do in the next hour?

4. Where am I letting comfort quietly steal my greatness?

5. If my discipline were a blade, am I sharpening it daily or letting it rust?

Chapter 13
The Achievement Sequence

*"Whatever the mind of man can conceive
and believe, he can achieve."*
—Napoleon Hill

There is a rhythm to greatness in any endeavor. A law hidden in plain sight, not reserved for the gifted or the privileged, but activated by those who understand how the inner world shapes the outer one. That rhythm is captured in three powerful words: *Conceive. Believe. Achieve.* This isn't a slogan. It's a blueprint for a timeless sequence that explains how ordinary people create extraordinary lives through self-mastery. It begins in the unseen and moves through the soul, ending up in a world where others can finally see what you already knew deep inside. A big point of life is to take chances on dreams that seem crazy to most, but feel like destiny to you.

It Starts with an Image

Every masterpiece begins with a mental picture. Before the architect draws the blueprint, he sees the building. Before the musician writes the song, she hears the melody in her spirit. Before you create the life you desire, you must conceive it in your imagination with clarity and courage. To conceive is to dare to see what doesn't yet exist by granting yourself permission to dream and envision what others might call impossible. This takes guts, as most people shrink their visions to fit their current circumstances. Those who master life expand their thinking to match their potential, not their present. Eleanor Roosevelt said it best - "The future belongs to those who believe in the beauty of their dreams." You can't achieve what you can't imagine. If your vision is blurry, your direction will be uncertain. Conceiving your ideal future is not wishful thinking; it's mental architecture. Every legendary achievement began with someone seeing it long before the world did.

Build the Inner Certainty

After conception comes the real test, and that is belief. This is where most people fall. They can imagine something better, but they don't believe it's for them. "He who says he can, and he who says he can't are both usually right." —Confucius. Doubt creeps in, and fear silences the voice of destiny. But belief isn't about wishing, it's about knowing, deep down, that what you've seen is possible and within your reach. Belief is the fuel that keeps your vision alive when nothing around you reflects it yet. It's the quiet confidence that whispers, "Keep going," when everything in the world says, "Give up." This kind of belief is cultivated, not automatic. You have to feed it through repetition, affirmation, surrounding yourself with possibility thinkers, and most importantly, small wins. Every time you keep a promise to yourself, you build self-trust. Every time you act in faith, your belief muscle grows stronger.

Become What You Saw

The final step, Achieve, is about taking action. "Action is the foundational key to all success." —Pablo Picasso. Achieving is not just about reaching a goal. It's about manifesting your full self in the real world, physical evidence of your mental and emotional alignment. It's the outer echo of the inner vision you held onto when no one else saw it. Achievement doesn't come from hustle alone, as it needs harmony. When your thoughts, beliefs, and actions are aligned, life begins to respond to you. Doors open, resources appear, and strength rises. But only if you move. Too many people conceive and believe, but stop just short of execution. They wait for perfect timing and overthink, or they let fear paralyze motion. Remember this truth that an imperfect action with belief will outperform perfect hesitation every time. Achievement demands movement.

Living the Formula Daily

This formula isn't just for mountaintop moments, as you can live it daily. Conceive how you want your day to feel and believe you have the strength and wisdom to handle it. Then act in alignment by moving with purpose and executing with excellence.

When you apply this to your relationships, your health, your finances and your calling, you become unstoppable. Not because you're perfect, but because you're aligned. Don't ask yourself if you're worthy of the dream. Ask if the dream is worthy of your life.

The Truest Law of Manifestation

So many people chase success without blueprinting it in their souls. They want results without building belief and applause without action. You'll stop chasing and start creating when you learn to master this law…Conceive. Believe. Achieve. Whatever you can see and believe, you are already halfway to achieving. Just remember: The world rewards courage aligned with vision.

Conceive your masterpiece and believe in it like your life depends on it, then achieve it by living one bold, faithful step at a time. You are not waiting for the future, but shaping it. Your most powerful tool is imagination under discipline. When you consistently see your best self, your deepest values, and your desired outcome, you become the architect of a life that cannot be shaken by circumstances. Vision rewrites identity and pierces through resistance, then summons the resources, the people, and the momentum you need to achieve that vision and belief.

Visualize, Then Walk

Tonight, before you sleep, close your eyes and picture your life a year from now if you lived every day with vision, discipline, and action. Not one day, but every day. Then tomorrow, do one thing that brings that vision closer. Repeat that rhythm daily and remember that the dream was planted in you for a reason. Seek to honor it by seeing it, believing in it, then becoming it.

No one embodies Napoleon Hill's law of "Conceive. Believe. Achieve." quite like Elon Musk. Decades before reusable rockets and self-driving cars were realities, Musk conceived them in vivid detail on paper, in late-night conversations, and in his relentless mind.

While most people saw the limits, physics, money, and ridicule, Musk saw possibilities. He dared to imagine a world where Mars was within reach, where sustainable energy powered entire cities, and where Artificial Intelligence could be harnessed for human benefit. But it didn't stop there. What set Musk apart was his unshakeable belief, even in the face of spectacular setbacks such as exploding rockets, near bankruptcy, and global skepticism.

When SpaceX rockets failed, when Tesla teetered on the brink, most would have retreated.

Musk doubled down, betting every dollar and ounce of energy on his vision. His belief wasn't naïve optimism, but a conviction so deep that it infected teams, moved markets, and rewrote what's possible. Finally, he took relentless action; working 100-hour weeks, sleeping on factory floors, and personally learning everything he didn't know. He didn't just dream, he built. In Musk's life, the blueprint is obvious: Conceive the impossible, believe in it until others catch on, and achieve it through unyielding action. He's proof that when your inner vision and outer effort align, you don't just predict the future, you can create it.

Tactical Tool: The CBA Loop

Every great thing is built over time, first in the mind, then in the world. The dream is the blueprint, belief is the foundation, and action is the hammer that makes it real. Most stop at dreaming, while some make it to belief. The few who keep swinging until the vision stands in front of them are the ones who change everything. Five questions to build and live your blueprint:

1. Have I fully pictured the result I want, down to the details?

2. Do I believe without condition that I can achieve it?

3. What bold step can I take today to bring my vision closer?

4. Who or what is eroding my belief, and how will I remove it?

5. If I acted every day as if my dream were inevitable, what would I do differently?

Chapter 14
The Ritual of Mastery

"We are what we repeatedly do. Excellence,
then, is not an act, but a habit."

—Aristotle

In the pursuit of self-mastery, grand visions and bold declarations are often celebrated, but it is our habits and rituals that quietly decide who we become. While goals give us direction, it is the systems of repeated actions, built into the rhythm of daily life, that carry us across the finish line. Your future is shaped by the habits you repeat, not goals that you set. As James Clear reminds us in *Atomic Habits,* "You do not rise to the level of your goals. You fall to the level of your systems." It's a truth echoed by ancient Stoics, elite athletes, spiritual sages, and high performers across generations…greatness is built, not declared.

Ritual is what gives form to our days and rhythm to our growth. It's how we take abstract values of discipline, gratitude, and courage and embody them. A ritual doesn't have to be elaborate; it can be as simple as beginning each day with silence with a moment of gratitude, a short workout, or a handwritten intention.

Over time, these practices become identity-shaping. If you journal daily, you become reflective. If you meditate each morning, you become mindful. If you write goals and review them weekly, you become focused. Ritual is repetition with meaning. And when you repeat with intention, you begin to reinforce a self-image that aligns with your highest potential.

Marcus Aurelius journaled privately, asking himself how to better live in accordance with nature, duty and reason. Epictetus taught his students to examine their actions daily and to prepare their minds each morning for the trials of the day. These rituals weren't done for show but were a form of self-check and a personal compass that keeps the inner life aligned with timeless virtues. Rituals give us a moment to return, to remember who we are, and who we are becoming.

James Clear's system-based philosophy bridges ancient wisdom with modern neuroscience. He shows how habits are not just behaviors, but feedback loops reinforcing identity. Want to be a writer? Write each day. Want to be fit? Train consistently. The key isn't intensity but consistency. "Every action you take," Clear says, "is a vote for the type of person you want to become." That's the core of self-mastery, casting intentional votes each day through simple repeated action. When our rituals and habits reflect our values, we become stable, focused and difficult to shake regardless of the circumstances around us.

Self-mastery is a quiet unfolding and a result of thousands of small decisions made deliberately, under the radar, before anyone notices. That's the power of habit and the glory of ritual. They are the invisible foundation behind every extraordinary life. Build your systems wisely, and you will not have to chase excellence but live inside of it.

Stephen King, one of the most prolific and celebrated authors of our time, didn't become a literary legend through sudden bursts of inspiration or grand declarations. He built his career and his identity on an unbreakable daily ritual, writing every single day.

Regardless of holidays, birthdays, or how he felt, King sat at his desk and wrote at least 2,000 words. This wasn't about waiting for the muse; it was about creating a system that made writing inevitable. King's process is famously simple - same time, same place, every day, until the work is done. He starts his mornings with a cup of tea, his vitamins, and music, and then he writes. Sometimes the writing flows; other times, it's a slog. But King doesn't debate with himself. The ritual is non-negotiable.

Over the years, this repeated discipline didn't just produce dozens of bestsellers and iconic stories, but also shaped his self-image. He doesn't just write books - he is a writer because he's built a system to embody that identity every single day. King has said, "Amateurs sit and wait for inspiration, the rest of us just get up and go to work."

His success is proof that excellence is not a lightning bolt, but a habit—one word, one page, one disciplined day at a time. The quiet ritual of daily writing became the architecture of an extraordinary career.

King didn't rise to the level of his goals; he fell back on the strength of his habits. Whether in writing, sports, leadership, or life, it is your systems, your daily habits and rituals, that decide your destiny. If you want excellence, don't chase it. Build it - one small, meaningful action at a time, until it's simply who you are.

Tactical Tool: The Ritual Alignment Blueprint

Friends have asked me how I wrote *Glorious Lethal Euphoria* without burning out or losing focus. The answer isn't motivation but ritual. Every morning started the same with a quiet moment before speaking to anyone, a quick burst of physical training, then an uninterrupted block of thinking, writing and editing with no phone, no noise, just the work. I journal daily to check my thinking, review my goals weekly, and protect my priorities with strict time blocks. You don't need to overhaul your life in a week. You need one ritual, done daily, that pulls you toward your best self. Stack those rituals over time, and excellence stops being something you chase. It becomes the air you breathe. Excellence doesn't happen by accident, as you become whatever you practice most. Five questions to shape your rituals:

1. If my habits were the only proof of who I am, what would they say about me?

2. Which daily action, if repeated for a year, would most transform my identity?

3. What current rituals are pulling me away from the person I want to be?

4. How can I design my environment so my desired habits are the easiest option?

5. If my future self could thank me for one habit I built this year, what would it be?

Shaping Thought Review

Chapters 6-14

The previous chapters push for harder, more reliable thinking patterns and behaviors that file your craft to a keener edge. Before we press on, let's stop and recap the last nine chapters. These are disciplines to practice until they live in your bones. The truisms you've read here have proven to work, and they matter now as much as ever. Human nature hasn't changed, so make these your fixed ground in a moving world. With that in mind, here's what you must embed, not just understand, before we continue our quest for self-mastery.

Develop your Creed: A creed of non-negotiables is a deliberate, uncompromising declaration of who you are and what you will live by, formed in conviction and proven in action. It demands radical ownership, calling you to train your thoughts, choose your attitude, guard your circle, and speak truth.

Your Inner and Outer Speak: Your self-talk is the silent conductor of your outcomes; eliminate the corrosive script of sarcasm and self-insult, and replace it with deliberate language that programs resilience, learning, and positivity. As you master this, you'll begin to feel the quiet success of focus, peace, and purpose as everyone around you will sense the moment you enter the room.

Speech and Body Language Congruence: Your gut often flags what words conceal because body language is the loudest channel, broadcasting intent and emotion before speech arrives. Learn to read that "second conversation" and you'll detect congruence or contradiction, calibrate your presence, guard boundaries, and influence ethically. When words and signals diverge, trust the body, because under stress or deception, it leaks truth even when language is scripted. Treat body language as a disciplined practice so you can read the room and connect with clarity and power.

Living Now: We squander life by ping-ponging between tomorrow's fears and yesterday's regrets, forgetting the present is the only place anything real can be lived, healed, or created. Real mastery is the courage to return and stay in the now. Practically, notice the body's signals, interrupt mental clutter, breathe, and re-anchor attention because the quality of your life is the quality of the moments you fully inhabit.

Audit Your Circle: Your character is heavily shaped by proximity, so align your circle with your values. Toxic companions sap confidence, blur boundaries, and choke out ambition as, over time, their repeated behaviors become your habits. High-character people, on the other hand, act by reinforcing belief, accountability, and resilience. Your circle is your ecosystem, so curate it with intention, and you'll be elevated into the person your values are calling forth.

Growth Requires Uncomfortableness: Avoidance isn't protection, but can quickly become procrastination, perfectionism, or an addiction. Keep in mind that what you resist, persists (Jung), and meaning is found by moving through suffering, not around it (Frankl). The Stoic path is blunt: stop running because what you confront becomes your servant, while what you evade becomes your master. Practically, face the hard conversation, take the first imperfect step, and dig up what you've buried until it loses its power—what you face, you free.

Discipline Isn't Punishment: Disciplined training hardens the soul to endure and govern itself, choosing what is right over what is easy and aligning actions with values. In practice, discipline is alignment. You rise early because the mission matters, and you say no to temptations not from deprivation but devotion to something higher. The resistance you feel is a compass pointing to your next level, so move now, because procrastination steals time.

Conceive, Believe, and Achieve: Lived daily, this sequence becomes imagination under discipline, and the world rewards that courageous alignment, not mere potential. First, you build a mental blueprint that dares to exceed current circumstances and gives your effort a destination. Next comes cultivating inner certainty so your vision survives dry seasons. Then, through aligned execution, take action, remembering that when you are faced with obstacles, they can be gifts and become opportunities. See it, believe it, then become it: visualize consistently and take one bold step each day until the future you pictured is the life you're living.

Establishing Rituals: Design rituals so easy you can't not do them. For example, silence at dawn, morning gratification, followed by physical workout and a weekly review to modify for better results. Let this repetition be design and with meaning reshape who you are. Build wisely and you won't have to chase excellence, you'll inhabit it, and steadily become the person your highest values predict.

Perspectives

Chapter 15
The Root of Abundance

———————— ◈ ————————

Gratitude clears the eyes of the soul, and the recognition of your gifts is another step toward wisdom. You are chosen and formed not by accident but by intention. Having faith in this is not weakness, but a beginning of strength, humility, and purpose.

When you understand that you were designed, not just evolved, something in your spirit steadies. Your gratitude deepens, and your capacity to endure and grow expands. Solomon reminds us constantly: "The fear of the Lord is the beginning of wisdom." (Proverbs 9:10) That is, true clarity begins not in pride or control, but in awe in reverence for something greater than yourself.

Gratitude is rooted in this understanding and is the natural response of a soul that realizes that you did not make yourself or earn every breath. You are here because of grace, not just grit. Without this posture of thankfulness, even the greatest success becomes hollow. We begin to think we are the architects of everything, and that delusion always leads to fear, insecurity, or arrogance. But when we recognize our advantages, such as where we were born, the mentors who showed up, the gifts wired into our being, we stop pretending we're self-made. That humility becomes another superpower. When you know you were given much, you feel compelled to give much, and you shift from entitlement to stewardship.

The Stoics called for living in alignment with nature, but what if that nature was written by a Creator with intention and love? Then life is not something to just survive, but to honor. Every moment becomes sacred, every trial becomes a test, and every advantage becomes an opportunity to serve, not to boast, when you combine faith in a Creator with the awareness of your blessings, life changes.

You stop asking, "Why me?" in suffering and start asking, "What is this teaching me?" You stop comparing and start building, stop drifting and start living with direction.

You were not meant to wander as a lost spark in a cosmic vacuum without meaning. You were made to reflect something eternal. When you live with gratitude and purpose, you stop chasing validation because you already know that you matter. You have a role to play; let that truth humble and elevate you. And let it remind you that the greatest way to thank the Creator is to fully become what He designed you to be.

Nick Vujicic was born without arms or legs, A reality that could have easily led to a life of bitterness, resentment, or self-pity. As a child and teenager, Nick often struggled with despair and the belief that his life was an accident, a cruel twist of fate. He asked the questions so many of us do in our darkest moments: "Why me?" "What purpose could my life possibly have?"

The world's messages of self-sufficiency and achievement seemed not just unreachable, but almost mocking. But everything changed when Nick began to shift his perspective, not through more striving, but through gratitude. He started to recognize the gifts in his life, like the love of his parents, the mind and spirit he'd been given, the opportunities to inspire others, and the profound resilience that grew from his adversity. He stopped measuring his worth by what he lacked and started recognizing what he had. He realized, "I did not make myself. My life is not meaningless. I am here for a reason."

With this new lens, Nick's world expanded. He developed a sense of stewardship over his story, using his struggles to serve others rather than hide in shame. His gratitude didn't deny pain; it clarified his vision and steadied his heart. Instead of being crushed by his circumstances, he became a world-renowned speaker, author, and encourager, impacting millions by embodying purpose, faith, and gratitude.

Nick's journey shows that gratitude is not a naïve denial of difficulty, but a courageous act that clears the "eyes of the soul." It anchors you to a deeper truth: You are not here by accident. You have gifts, even if they're not the ones you expected. Gratitude transforms your attitude from "Why me?" to "Thank you, now what can I do with what I've been given?" In that shift, you find not just peace, but the foundation of true wisdom and the courage to fulfill your purpose.

Nick Vujicic's life is living proof: When you choose gratitude even in the midst of struggle, you open your soul to clarity, faith, and the recognition that you were made for a reason. That is the beginning of all growth and the deepest kind of freedom.

Tactical Tool: The Gratitude Alignment Practice

There's a shift that happens when you stop seeing yourself as an accident and start seeing yourself as intentional. Gratitude becomes more than a polite reaction, but a lens through which you see life. Humility opens the door to wisdom. The greatest danger to our clarity is forgetting the Source and believing that everything we have is solely the product of our own effort. When you acknowledge your gifts, your blessings, and the unseen hands that shaped your path, you're no longer weighed down by entitlement or comparison. Instead, you're lifted by stewardship. You live not to prove your worth, but to honor it. Five questions to anchor your perspective:

1. If I truly believed I was created with intention, how would I live differently today?

2. What blessings or advantages in my life have I been taking for granted?

3. Where am I acting as though I am self-made, forgetting the people, moments, or grace that shaped me?

4. How can I turn gratitude into action and service this week?

5. What would my decisions look like if I saw every gift as a responsibility?

Chapter 16
The Journey Shapes What
The Destination Cannot

"It doesn't make sense to continue wanting something if you're not willing to do what it takes to get it. If you don't want to live the lifestyle, then release yourself from the desire. To crave the result but not the process is to guarantee disappointment."
—James Clear

For self-mastery, the process is being internally motivated through a disciplined commitment to do the right things, the right way, at the right time, with the right attitude, repeated daily, regardless of outcome. Progress comes by mastering effort, not controlling the result. It's not glamorous and it's not loud. It asks for no attention and gives no immediate reward. But it's the bedrock of inner strength.

My sales teams over the years knew the rule: "Have a ruthless focus on the process and bank the proceeds." The Stoics did not concern themselves with results beyond their control. They trained their minds and shaped their character through the repetition of virtuous behavior. This is the process. It strips away the illusion of control over fortune and places full responsibility on your choices. It is rising early when no one commands you to and doing your work with excellence, even when no one sees. It keeps your mind focused, your emotions in check, and your ego restrained. Through it, you become anchored and learn not to be ruled by emotion or tossed by external chaos.

This is why the process leads to self-mastery, as it requires you to govern yourself and do the hard things, not because they guarantee success, but because they align with who you want to become. You do not master the world by force, but you can master yourself by practice.

The man who follows the process becomes unshaken by praise or blame, by gain or loss. He does not ask, "Did I win?" but "Did I act with virtue?" In this, the process becomes not just a means of achievement, but a way of being, resulting in a quiet, relentless path to self-mastery.

The outcome is never fully yours to command, as there are too many variables, too much illusion of control. But you own your preparation, attention to detail, and the decision to do the right thing, the right way, the right time with the right attitude, regardless of what the scoreboard says.

Remember, you don't rise to the occasion, but sink to the level of your training. Time has only proven how true those words remain. Train your mind well relentlessly, intentionally, and with the quiet patience of someone who knows that greatness is found not in one grand moment, but in a thousand small decisions made with integrity.

Coach John Wooden never mentioned winning to his players. He taught them to focus on becoming the best version of themselves, every day, every practice, every possession. "Success," he said, "is peace of mind, which is a direct result of self-satisfaction in knowing you made the effort to become the best of which you are capable." That is process thinking by placing your energy and focus on what you can control, not what you hope to gain. It's easy to be results-obsessed, but wisdom lies in pursuing excellence regardless of results - although your results will probably exceed expectations.

Engaging the process isn't just about work ethic or performance; it is a moral compass, as you don't chase greatness, you align with it one decision at a time. When you live like that, you don't just perform well, you also live well. You become immovable in adversity, humble in victory, and consistent in every season of life. Because in the end, results fade. Headlines get recycled, but how you lived, worked, and carried yourself is what endures.

Managing the process rightly also does more than lead to success. It provides a daily test of who you are and who you're becoming. It teaches humility by reminding you that control lies only in your actions, not outcomes. It demands patience, because true growth cannot be rushed. It cultivates integrity, because shortcuts violate the very spirit of mastery. In truth, the process is the thread that ties together every principle in this book.

Whether we speak of discipline, resilience, self-awareness, communication, humility, or character, the process is the training ground where those virtues are forged. You don't develop wisdom by wishing for it or build grit by hoping for better days. These qualities are earned through consistent action guided by clear internal standards. That's what makes the process so powerful, as it becomes a way of life.

In choosing to live by this path, you are choosing a path where the inner scorecard matters more than the outer one. And when that becomes your standard, you will win far more often and lose far less deeply than those who chase outcomes without mastering themselves.

So, whether you're chasing greatness in business, sport, or simply the challenge of being a better human, remember that the process isn't a means to the end; it is the end. Master it and you'll never fear results again.

Both Coaches John Wooden and Nick Saban stand as living testaments to the power and primacy of the process. Wooden, the legendary UCLA basketball coach, never demanded championships from his players; instead, he demanded daily excellence through attention to details in practice, humility in preparation, and integrity in every action. For Wooden, the process was sacred. His focus wasn't on the scoreboard but on the unglamorous habits that built character and skill, such as tying your shoes right, practicing fundamentals, arriving early, and leaving better.

Similarly, Nick Saban's dynasty at Alabama's football program is not built on slogans or hype, but on a relentless commitment to the process, a system of disciplined, focused execution. Saban tells his players, "Don't look at the scoreboard. play the next play." For him, it's not about chasing victory, but about the habits, decisions, and attitudes that forge champions, snap by snap, day by day. Neither coach asks his team how they feel about the grind, as both remind them that mastery is born in what you repeat, not what you want.

The process demands you show up, regardless of outcome or mood, and that is where greatness is quietly built. Through the process, Wooden and Saban elevate sport into a laboratory of life, showing that real victory isn't the result, but who you become in pursuit of it. Their legacy proves the process doesn't care about your feelings, but it will reward your discipline, your growth, and, ultimately, your character.

Tactical Tool: The Process Tracker

Nick Saban doesn't win because he finds the right words on game day. He wins because of what happens every day before it. His players don't just practice plays; they practice process. Every meeting starts on time. Every drill is run at full speed, and repetition has a purpose. Saban defines the process as a relentless commitment to executing the smallest details with precision, over and over, until excellence becomes second nature. That's why his teams don't crumble under pressure as they've already lived that moment a thousand times in practice. Saban's genius is understanding that rituals create identity. You can't wait for big games or big opportunities to turn on your best self. Whether it's his morning routine, the structure of practice, or his meticulous review of film, Saban treats each habit like a brick in the wall of a championship legacy. The scoreboard takes care of itself when the habits are right. Five questions about installing your own well-oiled machine:

1. What non-negotiable routines in my life will guarantee I'm prepared before the big moments arrive?

2. Where am I letting "good enough" slip into my process?

3. If I approached each day like it was championship week, how would I behave differently?

4. What small detail, if done with Saban-level consistency, would transform my results?

5. Am I more focused on the outcome... or on perfecting the process?

Chapter 17
Even the Sun Returns After the Longest Night

"Though the righteous fall seven times, they rise again."
—Proverbs 24:16

Adversity is life's most honest instructor, and it does not flatter, apologize or ask permission. But it always leaves a mark, and whether that mark becomes a scar or a source of strength is up to us. The road to self-mastery is paved with difficulty, discomfort, and pressure. The most transformative growth doesn't come when things are easy, but when we are forced to face what we didn't think we could survive. It is in those moments that resilience is born as a way of being.

To understand resilience, we must first distinguish between two often-confusing ideas, grit and grind. Grit is purposeful persistence. It is suffering with meaning, endurance with alignment, a kind of inner toughness that stays connected to a deeper why. Grit is not about being a machine. It's about being deeply human and still choosing to continue. Grind is effort without vision. It's the glorification of exhaustion, a relentless hustle that too often leads to burnout and bitterness. Grind is mechanical, like survival on repeat. The difference is crucial as Grit builds you up and Grind wears you down.

We see Grit embodied in people who have turned unimaginable pain into purpose. Take David Goggins, abused, neglected, and broken as a child. He could have stayed a victim, but instead, challenged himself through brutal physical and mental challenges, like becoming a Navy SEAL, ultramarathoner and author. His journey was about mental transformation, by embracing suffering as a tool and using adversity as a furnace to build an indestructible mindset. He calls it the "calloused mind", not for show, but for survival and strength.

Jocko Willink, another modern warrior of resilience, speaks of ownership. A former Navy SEAL commander turned leadership coach, Jocko teaches that the first step to overcoming adversity is radical responsibility. His mantra, "Discipline equals freedom," is simple, but it hits hard. When the world falls apart, discipline becomes the foundation. In darkness, its structure that saves us. Both Goggins and Willink understand what many forget: Adversity is not the end of the road; it's the starting line for those willing to rise.

But beyond pushing through pain, there's something deeper, and that's post-traumatic growth. This is a powerful concept that flips the script. Instead of asking, "How do I recover?" we ask, "What can I build from this?" Studies show that many people who endure trauma don't just bounce back but bounce forward. They emerge stronger, more grounded and more purposeful than before. They gain a deeper appreciation for life, sharpened priorities, and greater spiritual or emotional depth. It is not that the trauma disappears; they grow around it. Like trees that wrap themselves around obstacles, they adapt, and in doing so, they become more resilient.

Post-traumatic growth is not about pretending the pain didn't happen. It's about integrating pain into your story in a way that gives it meaning. As Viktor Frankl said: "When we are no longer able to change a situation, we are challenged to change ourselves." That's the essence of growth through adversity…not erasing suffering but extracting the strength from it. Resilience, then, is not a trait you are born with. It's the skill of transforming suffering. Choose to treat failures as information, not embarrassment or shame, then losses become stepping stones. True self-mastery is not found in avoiding hard things but is developed through facing them head-on with courage and with the unshakable belief that life is not happening *to* you, it is happening for you.

So, when the storm comes, and it will, you don't need to panic. You need to plant your feet. Don't grind blindly. Grit it up with purpose. Don't just endure, evolve. Let pain be your teacher, not your prison. Resilience is not about bouncing back. It's about rising better.

Before her global success, J. K. Rowling's life was marked by what most would call repeated failure. She lost her mother to illness, endured a painful divorce, struggled with single motherhood, and lived on welfare, by her own account, as "poor as it is possible to be in modern Britain without being homeless."

During this time, she faced rejection after rejection from publishers, each one a door slammed in the face of her dream. But what defined Rowling wasn't the number of times she fell; it was the relentless way she rose each time. She continued to write in coffee shops while her daughter slept beside her. She revised her manuscript with grit and hope, undeterred by disappointment or discouragement.

Rowling's resilience didn't mean she never felt defeated or afraid. It meant she persisted anyway, aligning her efforts with the vision she carried in her soul. Eventually, her story was accepted, and Harry Potter became a cultural phenomenon, inspiring millions.

The world sees triumph, but the real victory was in the repeated rising. Rowling's journey transforms ancient wisdom into living proof - "It's not how many times you fall that shapes your destiny, but how many times you rise, carrying your scars as seeds of new strength." That's what true resilience looks like - falling, rising, and letting every setback refine rather than define you.

Tactical Tool: The Rise-Again Protocol

I've been knocked flat before. Not just inconvenienced…I mean gut-punched by life so hard it took the wind, the balance, and for a while, the will out of me. Times when the easiest thing to do would have been to stay down. But I learned that staying down is a choice. So is getting back up. For me, resilience wasn't built in a single, defining moment, but grew over years of small recoveries. Every setback, whether in business, relationships, health, or personal dreams, forced me to decide who I was going to be on the other side of it. I started asking myself a simple question whenever I hit the ground: "Am I going to let this be my story, or just a chapter in it? Will I let this define me? No!" Sometimes it's just getting up one more time, and you're there. It's standing in the storm with a purpose so strong that the wind can't move it. Five questions to activate your own Rise-Again Protocol:

1. When I'm on the floor, what's the *first small win* I can take that proves I'm still in the fight?

2. What part of this adversity can I turn into a skill, a lesson, or a strength?

3. Am I grinding without direction, or applying grit toward something that matters?

4. If my future self were watching me now, what would they want me to do next?

5. How can I grow around this challenge instead of just getting through it?

Chapter 18
What We Heal in the Child, We Free in the Soul

The child within us remembers the wounds. The soul within us is called to heal them by rising above them with love, meaning and wisdom. In the quest for self-mastery, emotional healing is part of the climb. Many people seek power, purpose, and success, but find themselves mysteriously blocked. They read books, do the work, speak the affirmations, yet progress feels like wading through invisible mud. That resistance often has nothing to do with intelligence or ambition. It may stem from something much deeper, buried in the subconscious. The unseen inner child is still carrying the pain, confusion and unmet needs of our earliest years.

Most avoid this layer as it's easier to push forward than to look back. But what we don't confront, we carry. The child within us doesn't disappear just because we grow up. In fact, the younger versions of ourselves often run the show through our triggers, fears, overreactions, people-pleasing, perfectionism or the belief that we are never enough. This is where self-mastery must tackle understanding.

Much of our identity is shaped in childhood. Family dynamics, early traumas, school conditioning and cultural expectations form the inner narrative we live by. We learn whether love is earned or freely given. We internalize whether we are safe to express emotion or whether we must hide it. We adopt silent beliefs like:

"I'm too much," "I'm not enough," "I must perform to be loved," or "My needs don't matter." These beliefs go unchecked for decades until, one day, they collide with our dreams. And we wonder why we sabotage the very things we say we want.

Many finally realize that healing the inner child isn't weakness, it's warrior work. It requires slowing down and listening to the part of you that never got the nurturing it needed. It means creating space in your adult life to re-parent yourself with compassion, patience, and truth. You begin to say to that little version of you: "You did the best you could. I see you. I'm here now. And I won't abandon you again." That inner safety becomes the foundation for everything else, emotional resilience, authentic confidence and the ability to connect without armor.

True self-mastery cannot be built on repression, as it must be rooted in integration. The Stoics spoke of knowing oneself. Viktor Frankl spoke of turning pain into meaning. Eckhart Tolle speaks of the "pain-body" we carry. All of them understood that our past is not our prison, but it must be acknowledged before it can be transformed. You cannot shame your inner child into strength. You must love it there. Because once that wounded part of you feels safe, it stops screaming, and in that silence, you'll hear your highest self speak with clarity, wisdom, and peace.

Healing old wounds is not about blaming, it's about reclaiming. When you bring light to the places you've hidden, you unlock the energy that has been trapped in fear, grief, or confusion. That energy becomes clarity, creativity, and confidence. That is self-mastery. So, go back if you truly want to rise. Not to stay there, but to retrieve the part of you left behind. The child who still needs to hear: You are worthy. You are enough. And you are free now.

Oprah Winfrey's childhood was marked by profound trauma through poverty, instability, and abuse. For years, she carried shame and self-doubt, believing she was unworthy of love and success. Despite her ambition and talent, those old wounds often surfaced as self-sabotage, anxiety, and a desperate need to please others. Her breakthrough didn't come from ignoring the past but from courageously facing it.

Through therapy, spiritual work, and compassionate self-reflection, Oprah learned to acknowledge the pain her inner child carried. She began to "re-parent" herself—giving herself the safety, affirmation, and love she never received as a child. She says, "What I know for sure is that healing happens when you choose to give compassion to the wounded child inside you." This emotional healing didn't erase her memories, but it freed her from being defined by them. It transformed her pain into empathy and wisdom, which became the foundations of her success and her unique ability to connect deeply with others.

Oprah's story is living proof that when you heal your inner child, you don't just find peace, you can unlock the clarity, confidence, and power needed for true self-mastery.

Tactical Tool: The Inner Child Integration Practice

If old wounds are steering your present, it's time to take back the wheel. These five questions will help you find the younger you who's still waiting to be seen and free them once and for all:

1. What pain from my past still shapes my reactions today?

2. If I could speak to my younger self, what would I tell them to help them feel safe and loved?

3. What silent beliefs about myself have gone unchallenged for years?

4. What would my life look like if I released those beliefs?

5. What daily action can I take to reassure the child in me that we are safe now?

Chapter 19
Every Breath Is on Borrowed Time

———————— ◈ ————————

We all know we're going to die, yet most of us live like we won't. In the ancient Stoic tradition, this truth wasn't avoided, but embraced. As mentioned towards the beginning of this book, Memento Mori, remember that you must die, wasn't a morbid phrase. It was a call to urgency and presence. It was meant to awaken, not depress. Seneca urged, "Let us prepare our minds as if we'd come to the very end of life." Not so we fear death, but so we might finally learn how to live.

Modern life anesthetizes us from death by hiding it behind hospital doors and polished caskets. But in doing so, we dull the raw power of its message that life is not a rehearsal. You don't get to try again, and if you wait until you feel ready, you will be waiting at the edge of your grave.

When you face death, your priorities sharpen. Petty arguments lose their appeal, and the fear of failure looks foolish. You begin to act from truth, not fear. You start living for impact. In his legendary Stanford commencement address, Steve Jobs said, "Remembering that you are going to die is the best way I know to avoid the trap of thinking you have something to lose." After surviving cancer initially and facing his own mortality, Jobs said it best: "Death is life's greatest change agent."

It clears out the old and makes way for the new you that stops pretending and starts becoming. In Buddhist philosophy, *Anicca* is one of the three marks of existence. Nothing lasts, everything changes, and an attachment to what will inevitably pass is the root of suffering.

But viewed through the right lens, this awareness is not bleak, but beautiful. The cherry blossoms are precious because they fade. Your time on earth is sacred because it is limited. Every sunrise, every hug, every chance to forgive or create or speak your truth becomes priceless when you know it may be your last.

Contemplate the paradox of mortality: The more you deny it, the more you live in fear. Conversely, the more you accept it, the more courageous, focused, and alive you become. When you stop pretending you have endless time, procrastination dies, perfectionism dies, and approval addiction dies. What's left is clarity, truth and the life you were meant to live.

Memento Mori is not about thinking of death to be afraid, but about thinking of death to wake up. To finally stop waiting for permission, to have the conversation or launch the vision. To walk away from the life that no longer fits and step boldly into the one that does. You want self-mastery? Look death in the eye and thank it for the reminder, then live like today actually matters because it does.

Steve Jobs was already a visionary, but it was facing his mortality that brought his greatest clarity. In his 2005 Stanford commencement speech, given less than a year after he was diagnosed with pancreatic cancer, Jobs spoke openly about how his brush with death transformed his perspective on life, work, and meaning. He admitted: "When I was 17, I read a quote that went something like: 'If you live each day as if it was your last, someday you'll most certainly be right.'" For decades, he said, he looked in the mirror every morning and asked himself: "If today were the last day of my life, would I want to do what I am about to do today?" If the answer was "no" for too many days in a row, he knew he needed to change something. But the philosophy became real, not theoretical, when he received his cancer diagnosis. Suddenly, the finite nature of time was no longer an abstract idea; it was the only reality.

Jobs said, "Remembering that I'll be dead soon is the most important tool I've ever encountered to help me make the big choices in life. Because almost everything—all external expectations, all pride, all fear of embarrassment or failure—these things just fall away in the face of death, leaving only what is truly important." Jobs went on to explain that, for him, the awareness of mortality:

- *Killed his tendency to procrastinate or play it safe.*

- *Gave him the courage to follow his heart, even when it meant going against the crowd.*

- *Made him ruthlessly honest about what truly mattered, both in business and in relationships.*

- *Inspired him to pour his creative energy into work that he loved, rather than simply chasing money or status.*

He called death "life's change agent." Rather than being a reason to despair, he saw it as a force that "clears out the old to make way for the new." He urged the graduates not to "live someone else's life," or "be trapped by dogma, which is living with the results of other people's thinking." Instead, he said, "Your time is limited, so don't waste it living someone else's life." This is the heart of Memento Mori: When you keep your own mortality close, you live braver, more honestly, and more fully. You let go of the illusion of endless tomorrows and, paradoxically, that's what lets you live with urgency, presence, and real joy. Jobs's legacy was not just innovation; it was the radical clarity he modeled: Face death, and you'll finally see what is worth your life. Face death, and you'll act on what matters, while you still can.

Tactical Tool: The Memento Mori Practice

There have been moments when the fragility of my existence hit me like a cold wind, reminding me that nothing is promised. In those flashes, the noise falls away, excuses dissolve, and what matters sharpens into focus. Mortality strips away the illusion of "someday," pushing us to start the project, mend the relationship, speak the truth, and discard the busywork that fills days but empties life. Every breath is on loan. Every conversation, opportunity, and sunrise is part of a finite count we'll never know until the last one is gone. The only sane response is to live each day as if it's the most valuable you'll ever have—because it might be. Five questions to live the Memento Mori Mandate:

1. If I knew today was my last, what would I regret not starting?

2. Who needs to hear something from me before it's too late?

3. What am I postponing that matters more than my reasons for delaying?

4. If fear of failure vanished, what would I do differently *right now*?

5. Am I spending my life on what truly matters, or just passing time?

Chapter 20
The Poverty of Pleasure

"He who loves pleasure will become poor, and whoever loves wine and oil will never be rich."
—Proverbs 21:17

Focus holds your life steady, and when you lose it, what often looks like harmless escape becomes quiet self-destruction. The human spirit was not designed to wander aimlessly. In the absence of vision, the soul will search for sensation. And pleasure, while tempting, immediate, and dampening, is often the first thing it finds.

When the mind lacks purpose, it seeks relief. And the world is more than ready to offer it in the form of distractions and addictive behaviors. A drink to take the edge off. A pill to feel normal. A screen to forget. What begins as a break soon becomes a habit, and what was once a reward becomes a requirement.

Pleasure itself is not evil. The Stoics did not hate joy, nor does wisdom forbid laughter. But pleasure sought as a replacement for meaning becomes poison wrapped in sugar. Substance abuse, toxic relationships, gambling, pornography, and bingeing are not merely vices. They are symptoms of the loss of self-command.

When the mind is untrained, it craves comfort over growth, with comfort becoming a prison. Self-mastery begins where indulgence ends and won't negotiate with weakness. It requires you to sit with

128

discomfort, to resist the easy escape, to feel your feelings instead of sedating them. But it takes practice, vigilance, and the relentless return to your higher aim. "Do not join those who drink too much wine or gorge themselves on meat, for drunkards and gluttons become poor, and drowsiness clothes them in rags." —Proverbs 23:20.

Distraction is not just a waste of time; it is a theft of your potential and your inner peace. No one steals more from you than pleasure when it is pursued without purpose. As Robert Green says, "Your mind is like a muscle; it grows stronger the more it resists temptation and distraction." Your higher self is not found at the bottom of a bottle or in the haze of a dopamine loop. It is developed in resistance, sacrifice and in the courageous act of saying no when the world screams yes.

Growth is painful, and that's why most people choose to remain the same. But the price of stagnation is regret. The man who seeks pleasure today without restraint will wake up tomorrow with nothing to show but broken habits, broken promises and a broken will.

We have mastered the art of excuse-making by cloaking our stagnation in false self-care, masking fear as rest and dressing indulgence up as "deserved." But the truth is simpler and sharper than we'd like to admit.

Most people don't grow because they'd rather feel good than become great. Pleasure, in most of its forms, is not evil, but when it becomes a daily prescription for escaping discomfort, it transforms from reward into restriction. When you say, "I just need to unwind," what are you really saying or asking... Is the weight of growth too heavy? That facing your fears too exhausting? That pushing toward your purpose isn't worth the stress?

Pleasure becomes the excuse of the undisciplined. The path to mental, personal and professional evolution is not paved with chemical pleasure hits. It's lined with delayed gratification, trial, structure, humility, and a willingness to confront your own mediocrity. You cannot fill a spiritual void with sensual escape. No amount of scrolling, snacking, sipping, or sleeping in will make you the person you're called to be. And yet the default mode of the modern mind is to avoid discomfort, escape effort and rationalize idleness.

The excuse sounds like this: "I've had a long day. I deserve this." "Life's too short not to enjoy myself." "I'll get serious tomorrow." But tomorrow never arrives, as every time you choose pleasure over progress, you reinforce the neural path of weakness. You train your brain to chase ease rather than excellence. You wire yourself for decay, not development.

You do not deserve pleasure you have not earned. Not when you still haven't read the books that will shape you or when you've skipped the work that will free you. Not when you're avoiding the pain that will transform you. Let the world become detached, and the average person seek only to feel good. You must rise above the lie that pleasure equals peace by realizing peace comes not from sedation, but from integrity and knowing you are growing, rising and advancing toward your highest self.

The next time you reach for pleasure as a pacifier, pause and ask yourself, "Am I celebrating progress or escaping pressure?" If it's the latter, put it down and pick up your purpose. You are called to remember: Every time you resist unhealthy pleasure, you strengthen your resolve and sharpen your mind. Every time you say "not today" to a destructive urge, you reclaim your throne. This is the path of Glorious Lethal Euphoria.

Whitney Houston was often called "The Voice" and blessed with one of the most powerful and beautiful singing talents of all time. She broke records, inspired millions, and seemed destined for a lifetime of musical greatness.

Early in her career, Houston's discipline and focus led to a string of hit albums, Grammy Awards, and blockbuster films. She had everything - talent, opportunity, beauty, and global admiration. But as her fame grew, so did the pressures and temptations.

Whitney's life increasingly revolved around pleasure-seeking escapes such as drugs, alcohol, toxic relationships, and the numbing world of celebrity excess. What started as "fun" soon became a dependency. She became entangled in a cycle of substance abuse, missed performances, public breakdowns, and mounting professional and personal losses. Her once-soaring voice began to falter, and her reputation was tarnished by tabloid scandals.

Despite several attempts at recovery and brief comebacks, Houston's struggle with addiction and lack of a steady, purposeful foundation ultimately cost her everything. In 2012, she died tragically at just 48 years old, her talent and promise lost long before her time.

Whitney Houston's life shows that talent, opportunity and potential can all be wasted if focus is lost and pleasure becomes the guiding force. No matter how much someone is given, chasing escape over purpose, and comfort over self-mastery, leads only to loss: of wealth, health, relationships, legacy, and sometimes life itself. Her story is a sobering, human reminder that even the most gifted among us are not immune to the silent dangers of unchecked pleasure and loss of purpose. Without discipline and vision, potential turns into tragedy.

Tactical Tool: The Pleasure Audit

I've learned that every time I say "yes" to empty pleasure, I'm saying "no" to progress. And the scary part is that the brain gets used to it. It rewires itself for ease instead of excellence. Now, I guard my focus like my life depends on it, as it does. If I haven't done the work, pleasure can wait. Purpose comes first. Five questions to sharpen your resistance:

1. Is this pleasure a celebration of progress or an escape from the pressure to grow?

2. What am I avoiding right now by choosing comfort?

3. How would my future self judge the decision I'm about to make?

4. If this habit became permanent, would it build me or break me?

5. Am I stronger for having done this or weaker?

Chapter 21
The Silent Killer of Dreams

"You must protect your mind against distraction as you would your body against harm. For a mind scattered is a life lost."
—Marcus Aurelius

While we have unparalleled access, convenience, and connectivity, we have never been so scattered, anxious, and unfocused. Many of our most precious resources are being hijacked by a trillion-dollar economy built on tricking the chemicals and processes running our brains.

Dopamine is the brain's "reward" chemical. It's not pleasure itself but the anticipation of pleasure. Every ping, scroll, like, reel, or TikTok clip floods the brain with tiny hits of dopamine. Over time, our minds become addicted not to the reward but to the chase. This is why you can find yourself endlessly scrolling without joy, checking notifications you don't care about and feeling strangely drained after hours of consumption. You've been trained not by choice, but by design.

Big Tech engineers know this, as these platforms aren't just digital playgrounds but behavioral casinos. Algorithms prey on your need for novelty, and the brain responds like it's gambling: "Maybe the next scroll will be something amazing," and so the loop continues. The truth that most don't want to admit is that you must master your attention to master your life.

Self-mastery in the modern world requires a new skillset called digital self-mastery. It's the discipline to reclaim your mind in a world that profits from your distraction. It's the power to say my focus is mine, my peace is mine, and my time is sacred. Because if you don't guard it, someone else will gladly spend it for you.

Neuroscience shows us that overexposure to dopamine-inducing content, especially short-form video, rewires the brain. It shrinks your attention span, increases impulsivity and diminishes your capacity for deep thought, focus, and creativity. This is not just a minor inconvenience but a spiritual threat. The more distracted you are, the further you drift from your purpose and start reacting to life instead of designing it.

The good news is that what technology wires in, discipline can wire out. You can reset your brain and build what I call dopamine discipline, the daily practice of controlling your exposure, delaying gratification and choosing depth over noise. It starts small by silencing notifications, deleting apps you mindlessly check and creating screen-free blocks of time.

Replace doom-scrolling with intentional action, such as journaling instead of scrolling, walking instead of binging or meditating instead of consuming. These habits don't just protect your focus but rebuild your identity.

When you stop flooding your brain with artificial dopamine spikes, you regain sensitivity to the deeper, more fulfilling rewards of life, including creativity, calm, real relationships and spiritual clarity. These are not fast pleasures, but they are lasting. And they can't be captured in a 15-second clip.

Those who can learn to focus in a distracted world have the inside track to self-mastery. They will write the books, build the empires, form the strongest families, and experience a level of peace that the scrolling masses will never taste. Digital self-mastery is the gateway to real clarity, purpose and power. In the end, your ability to focus on what matters by ignoring what doesn't, will define the quality of your life. No one can do that work for you but you.

Tristan Harris was once a Google design ethicist, a Silicon Valley insider tasked with understanding how to make technology more engaging. He saw firsthand how teams of engineers and designers worked obsessively to perfect the "infinite scroll," notification badges, and algorithmic feeds that are all carefully crafted to maximize user engagement.

Harris and his colleagues knew the science that every ping, like, and swipe was a dopamine trigger, making it harder and harder for users to put their phones down. But as Harris began to see the psychological toll these features were taking, not just on users, but on himself, he grew uneasy. He noticed how his own attention, focus, and even sense of self were being fragmented by the endless chase for digital rewards. He watched friends, colleagues, and eventually, millions of people around the world become increasingly anxious, distracted, and addicted to their screens. The pursuit of convenience and novelty, powered by AI-driven algorithms, was making people less present, less creative, and more reactive.

The tipping point came when Harris realized: "If you don't control your attention, someone else will." He left Google and founded the Center for Humane Technology, warning the world about the dangers of tech-driven distraction and the erosion of focus. Harris became the central figure in the Netflix documentary, The Social Dilemma, *where he explained how algorithms are designed not for your well-being, but for your attention and ultimately, for profit. He showed how even the creators of these technologies fell prey to the same dopamine-driven loops as everyone else. In the age of Artificial Intelligence, attention is your most valuable resource. The platforms that promise connection and creativity can, if left unchecked, turn you into a pawn in a global experiment in distraction.*

Tristan Harris's journey from designer of digital traps to advocate for digital self-mastery proves that only by setting strong boundaries, cultivating focus, and practicing "dopamine discipline" can you reclaim your life from the machine.

If a Google ethicist, surrounded by the smartest minds and latest technology, could lose his focus to engineered distraction, anyone can. And if you want to thrive, not just survive, in the coming era of AI, you must learn to master your attention. Because those who can focus deeply in a distracted world will shape the future; those who can't, will be shaped by it. In the end, digital self-mastery is not just about productivity. It's about becoming the author of your own mind in a world that profits from writing your story for you.

In the coming years, your boss may be an algorithm that never sleeps. The news you read may be tailored to push your emotions toward outrage or complacency. Entire industries will appear and vanish in months, leaving careers and identities in their wake. Self-mastery is no longer a philosophical luxury but a survival skill in an age of invisible influence.

Tactical Tool: The Dopamine Discipline Protocol

As technology continues to evolve and steal your attention, focus isn't a break from distraction, but a fortress you build and defend daily. *Glorious Lethal Euphoria* exists because I carved out time, guarded it like sacred ground, and shut the door on the trivial. Boundaries are protection for what matters. Deep work, deep love and deep living survive only in a guarded mind. Say no to almost everything so you can say yes to what's essential. The ability to go deep is the foundation of a meaningful life. Five questions to strengthen your focus fortress:

1. If my attention were a bank account, whose spending it without permission?

2. What's the single biggest distraction that quietly pulls me away from my purpose each day?

3. When in my day am I most mentally sharp, and how can I guard that time fiercely?

4. What physical or digital boundaries could I set today to make focus my default state?

5. If my life were judged only by what I consistently focus on, would I be proud?

Chapter 22
Forgive, Remember, Rise

———————— ◈ ————————

Forgiveness is not forgetting but releasing the anchor so the soul may rise. Emotional mastery is remembering who you are, not what was done to you. Self-mastery isn't just about waking up early, setting goals, and grinding through resistance. It's also about the quiet, unseen battles, the emotional scars we carry and the pain we bury deep. You can have the perfect morning routine, a shredded calendar, and a full bank account, but if your heart is chained to bitterness, regret, or past betrayal, your growth is capped. Emotional baggage is real and it's heavy.

What we don't process emotionally, we shoulder energetically. Unforgiven wounds become weights that pull us backward when we try to rise. Anger that isn't faced becomes cynicism. Regret turns to shame, and jealousy breeds scarcity. These are blockages, not just emotions. They silently sabotage relationships, clarity, joy and purpose. Mastery demands not just discipline of the body and mind but liberation of the heart.

Forgiveness is the key. But let's be clear, forgiveness is not about approving someone else's behavior. It's not saying, "What happened was okay." It's not about letting someone else off the hook. Forgiveness is about liberating yourself. It's saying: "I refuse to carry this poison any longer." Resentment is a slow-drip toxin that steals your energy, your focus and your peace. This doesn't mean it's easy because sometimes we grip our pain like armor. We believe that holding onto the anger protects us from future hurt. But in reality, it keeps us stuck in an old story. Forgiveness is spiritual strength. It's not forgetting, but remembering without letting it define us.

Often, we need to forgive others, but just as often, we need to forgive ourselves. For the times we didn't know better or the opportunities we missed. For the words we wish we'd said or the ones we wish we hadn't. Your emotions are not the enemy, but they are signals. Anger shows where your boundaries were crossed, regret shows what mattered, and jealousy shows what you secretly desire. But if you process those emotions by suppressing them or deadening them with distraction, they harden into habits and rule you from the shadows.

Healing begins with compassion, not only for others, but especially for yourself. Speak to your past self with love, not shame and face your pain with courage, not avoidance. As Carl Jung said, "Until you make the unconscious conscious, it will direct your life, and you will call it fate."

Forgiveness brings the unconscious into light and gives you your power back, as when you're no longer weighed down by what was, you become unstoppable. You stop reacting, start responding, stop seeking validation and start creating meaning. You stop dragging the past into the present and start building the future with full power.

Emotional mastery is not about never feeling anger or sadness but about being the conductor of your inner orchestra, not the captive of your triggers. It's about knowing your freedom is one choice away, to forgive, to release, and to rise.

Nelson Mandela spent 27 years imprisoned under South Africa's brutal apartheid regime. He lost his youth, his freedom, and his family life, and witnessed horrific injustices. It would have been understandable, even expected, for Mandela to leave prison consumed by rage, seeking vengeance on those who had robbed him of so much.

Many people in his position remained chained to bitterness for the rest of their lives. But Mandela made a different choice. He understood that if he held onto hate and resentment, he would never truly be free, even outside the prison walls. In his own words: "As I walked out the door toward the gate that would lead to my freedom, I knew if I didn't leave my bitterness and hatred behind, I'd still be in prison."

Mandela's act of forgiveness wasn't an approval of what had been done to him or his people. It was an act of self-liberation, by making a conscious decision to release the poison of resentment so he could lead his nation, and his own life, with clarity and compassion. He forgave his jailers, negotiated with former enemies, and invited all South Africans into a future of reconciliation rather than revenge. This didn't mean he forgot the pain or denied the injustice.

Instead, he remembered without letting those memories chain him to victimhood. He chose peace over anger, hope over cynicism, and became an example to the world that forgiveness is not a weakness, but the highest strength.

Mandela's story is proof that holding onto anger keeps us anchored to the past, no matter our outer circumstances. Forgiveness, on the other hand, releases the soul to rise. It gives you your power back, not by erasing what happened, but by choosing who you become next.

Emotional mastery isn't about erasing scars, but about letting them become signs of wisdom, resilience, and compassion. As Mandela showed, forgiveness is the ultimate act of self-mastery and the key to content, purposeful living.

Tactical Tool: The Forgiveness Release Protocol

You can't run toward your future if you're dragging the weight of your past. Bitterness, regret, and resentment may feel like armor, but they're chains. Forgiveness isn't approval, it's release. It's choosing to cut the rope that keeps you tied to pain, not because they deserve it, but because you do. Until you do, every victory will feel heavy, every step forward slowed. Five questions to free your heart:

1. What grudge or regret is stealing my energy right now?

2. If I forgave fully, others or myself, what would my life feel like?

3. Am I holding onto this pain to protect myself, or to punish someone?

4. What lesson can I take from the hurt, so it becomes fuel, not poison?

5. If freedom is one choice away, what's stopping me from making it today?

Chapter 23
What You Didn't Do Will Haunt You

———————— ◈ ————————

In the end, the greatest burden is not what we suffered, but what we failed to do. Regret is the interest paid on time wasted. One day, your body will lie still, your breath will be gone, and your eyes will close for the final time. In that moment, you won't be thinking about your income, titles or your social media followers. You'll be thinking about the life you lived or the one you didn't. And nothing hits harder in that final hour than the silent ache of regret. Not regret for what happened, but for what you allowed not to happen. Regret doesn't strike like lightning, but festers like rust. You won't notice it at first as it shows up in whispers: "I should have said it," "I should have tried," "I should have walked away sooner."

The Stoics called this the tragedy of misused reason…when a person knows the right thing but fails to act. Seneca reminds us, "While we wait for life, life passes." And Proverbs cautions, "The sluggard does not plow in season, so at harvest time he looks but finds nothing." The lesson is clear; inaction today is scarcity tomorrow.

In your personal life, regret comes not from loving too much but from loving too late. From holding grudges when you could have made peace. From biting your tongue when you should have spoken the truth. While life is momentary, and relationships are our proving ground, don't wait for a tragedy to remind you of someone's worth. Say what needs to be said and forgive where you can. Leave where you must. As Proverbs (18:21) says, "The tongue has the power of life and death, and those who love it will eat its fruit." Choose your words with courage, not cowardice, as silence has a cost.

Professionally, regret looks like comfort disguised as success. It looks like staying at a job that kills your spirit because the benefits are "decent." It looks like not starting the business, not making the ask, not trusting yourself to step into your full potential.

Too many people die with their music still in them, not because they weren't talented, but because they feared rejection or failure more than regret. "He who gathers crops in summer is a prudent son, but he who sleeps during harvest is a disgrace," Proverbs warns. You are in your harvest season now, so don't sleep through it.

Let's be clear, regret doesn't only come from what you didn't do. Sometimes it comes from what you did, but for the wrong reasons. One of the most soul-crushing forms of regret is realizing you lived a life that wasn't even yours. You chased titles that didn't fulfill you and said "yes" when your soul screamed "no." You performed to impress, to be seen, to be applauded, only to find the applause fades and the emptiness echoes louder than ever.

Marcus Aurelius warned, "It never ceases to amaze me how we all love ourselves more than other people but care more about their opinion than our own." You cannot serve two masters, those being your inner truth and the expectations of others. Living for validation is slavery in disguise. And when the crowd moves on, you're left with the cost of your time, your energy and your purpose spent building someone else's idea of success.

In brutal honesty, most people won't remember you for what you tried to look like. They'll remember if you lived with fire, with love, with honor, or if you played it safe, small, and soulless. Do not sacrifice your soul to gain a round of applause from people who wouldn't show up to your funeral. That's the most expensive transaction you'll ever make. Ask yourself, "What have I been doing just to impress others? What parts of my life are performance, not purpose?" And more importantly, "What would my life look like if I stopped seeking to fit in and started living to stand out in truth?" Oscar Wilde said it best – "Be yourself; everyone else is already taken."

When you look back from your final days, may it not be with the bitter taste of a life filtered through fear or applause. Let it be with peace, knowing you had the courage to live boldly, love freely, work meaningfully and speak truthfully, for yourself, not for the gallery. Because in the end, your life is yours alone to live, but the regret of not doing so will be your heaviest burden.

So how do you avoid regret? You live intentionally and guard your time like it's gold. You make decisions that align with your values and creed, not your impulses, by saying "yes" to what builds your soul and "no" to what erodes it. You understand, as Epictetus wrote, "How long are you going to wait before you demand the best for yourself?" The answer is not one day longer. On your deathbed, you'll wish you had used the time you were given. You'll think of the chances you didn't take, the forgiveness you withheld, the love you didn't express and the life you lived at half-volume. Don't wait until your final breath to realize you were holding it the whole time. Breathe now, act now and speak now because the only thing more painful than failure is regret for never trying. Make sure your life is full of "I can't believe I did that" instead of "I wish I had done that."

Kurt Cobain changed the face of music. He brought raw emotion, vulnerability, and authenticity to a generation starved for truth. But behind the fame and creative brilliance, Kurt struggled deeply. He battled addiction, depression, and a sense that he was living a life dictated by others' expectations, fans, media, and the music industry.

Despite his outward success, Cobain felt trapped by the machine he helped create. In the note he left behind, Cobain confessed to living with a sense of emptiness and disconnection. He felt like he was performing, not living, by chasing approval and validation, yet never feeling worthy or truly known. He wrote of feeling "guilty beyond words" for not being able to enjoy the very things others assumed would bring happiness: family, art, and success.

At the heart of his sadness was a profound regret for the way he allowed fear, addiction, and other people's voices to dictate his choices. He wrote: "I don't have the passion anymore . . . I feel guilty for all of this. For not living up to what people expect of me . . . When we're backstage and the lights go out and the roar of the crowd begins, it doesn't affect me the way it did for Freddie Mercury, who seemed to love and relish the love and adoration from the crowd, which is something I totally admire and envy." His regrets weren't about fame or money, but about missing out on the simple joys of being present, being honest and being free to live his own truth.

Cobain's death at 27 was not just the loss of a musical genius, but a warning to all of us: The greatest pain at the end is not what we endure, but what we never allowed ourselves to try, express, or become. The applause fades, but regret for unlived life endures. His story is a sobering reminder that followers, titles, and external rewards are no replacement for a life lived intentionally, authentically, and fully.

Regret is not just sadness for the past; it's the soul's cry for the life you might have lived if you'd had the courage to be true, to speak up, to step out, to love and create without apology. Cobain's legacy compels us to seize the time we have, to act boldly, and to shape a story we'll be at peace with in our final hour, not one we mourn for what was left undone.

Tactical Tool: The Regret Prevention Protocol

Regret often arrives when it's too late to fix. And while we can recover from mistakes, we rarely escape the sting of what we never tried, never said or never dared. The only cure is intentional action now before the clock runs out. Five questions to silence regret before it starts:

1. If I died a year from today, what would I wish I had done differently?

2. Who do I need to forgive or tell I love before time runs out?

3. What dream or goal have I been postponing out of fear?

4. Where am I living for approval instead of alignment?

5. If I stopped waiting and acted today, what would my first step be?

Perspectives Review

Abundance through Gratitude: People experience "more" when they practice gratitude because it rewires attention toward what's working, reduces scarcity anxiety, and catalyzes behaviors (connection, generosity, perseverance) that actually create more opportunities, resources, and well-being. Mentally invest and live with a mindset of gratitude, and you will find that abundance in all parts of your life will be your ROI (Return on Investment)..

Mastering the Journey Matters: The process becomes the anchor that steadies your mind and emotions amid chaos. Being internally motivated to practice the right thing, the right way, at the right time with the right attitude, drives self-mastery. Your focus and shying away from the scoreboard destroys the moment, increases pressure and results in poor performance. Too much focus on the end result or "prize" adversely affects your confidence and self-esteem.

Facing Adversity: Life's hardest seasons tell the plain truth about us in that we can crack, or we can be carved into something stronger. Falling is inevitable; rising is a decision made in the quiet moments when you refuse to let pain write the last line. Real resilience isn't noisy grind but grit with purpose…effort steered by a why.

Your Inner Child Can Still Hold You Back: Many chase success and do the work yet feel mysteriously stuck because the real resistance lives in the subconscious as an unseen inner child carrying unmet needs and confusion. Left unaddressed, that early conditioning writes our adult script, and we end up sabotaging the very goals we claim to want. The courageous move is not to power through but to re-parent yourself. Healing doesn't change your past, but it does change your future.

Remember to Live: Face mortality head-on, not to brood, but to wake up to what matters now. Memento Mori is a discipline of urgency and presence, as life is not a dress rehearsal, and postponing until you're "ready" is a quiet form of self-betrayal. Remembering death dissolves the illusion of loss, clearing space to become who you truly are. Accept finitude, then watch procrastination, perfectionism, and approval-seeking wither, while meaningful purpose, contentment and existence expand.

Pleasure First Living: This lifestyle can hollow out both wealth and character. Ancient wisdom warns that unchecked indulgence corrodes prosperity. When direction fades, appetite takes the wheel, and what begins as harmless relief hardens into dependency. Joy isn't the enemy, but using sensation to plug a meaning-shaped hole becomes a sweet poison, and compulsions become the dashboard lights of surrendered self-command.

Digital Distraction: Guard your attention as you would your physical safety, because a scattered mind can slowly forfeit a whole life. A vast attention economy exploits your brain's reward circuits by hooking you on anticipation and chasing the next adrenaline hit. These loops shorten your span of focus, causing an erosion that is as spiritual as it is cognitive. The antidote is a disciplined digital strategy of self-governance that makes neuroplasticity work in your favor. For you to lower artificial stimulation, you regain sensitivity to life's richer rewards.

Forgive and Move On: Forgiving isn't erasing memory; it's cutting the rope to the anchor so your spirit can lift and remember who you are beyond what happened. You can have immaculate routines and impressive results, yet if you're clutching bitterness, regret, or betrayal, your ceiling lowers, unprocessed hurt turns into drag, cynicism, shame, and scarcity. To forgive is not to excuse; it's to stop drinking the poison yourself. Anger and resentment, worn as armor, can only trap you in yesterday's story.

The Deepest Pain: The heaviest load at life's end is rarely what hurts us, but the chances we never took, and the awareness of mortality strips that truth bare. Regret compounds quietly through every "I'll do it later," a misuse of judgment the ancients warned against. Today's laziness becomes tomorrow's emptiness. In love and friendship, what stings is loving too late. Beware of living by other people's scripts and choose your inner standard over the crowd's approval.

Responsibilities

Chapter 24
The Currency of Impact

---◆---

Proof of inner strength is not control, but contribution. True mastery transcends self and becomes a light others can follow. There comes a moment in a man's or woman's journey where the climb to personal achievement, growth, self-mastery and power brings them to a peak.

From that peak, they are gifted with a new vantage point, one that looks outward instead of inward. Self-mastery, it turns out, does not end with the self. In the beginning, the quest is survival, then it becomes success and then excellence. But the highest form of self-mastery is service, not out of obligation, but out of overflow. It's when your cup is so full that you must pour into others. This is where legacy is born.

When the focus of life shifts from "me" to "we," everything changes. Your choices no longer end at your personal gain, and your actions ripple into communities, generations, and unseen futures. The ego quiets and the soul begins to speak. You begin by asking yourself:

- Who am I helping?

- What am I building that will outlive me?

- What will people say about my character when I'm gone?

This shift is powerful. It matures you and deepens your sense of fulfillment in a way that money, titles, or applause never can. True fulfillment doesn't come from what you gather, but from what you give away.

Contribution is not just about charity or generosity, but about impact. It's using what you've mastered to lift others out of struggle, confusion, or darkness. You don't need to be perfect. You just need to be intentional with your strengths. Ask yourself:

- What pain have I overcome that others still suffer with?

- What knowledge have I gained that could accelerate someone else's path?

- What part of my story could bring someone hope?

This is how impact becomes currency as your wisdom, energy, and scars become tools to build something bigger than yourself.

The Sacred Power of Legacy

"The meaning of life is to find your gift. The purpose of life is to give it away."—**Picasso.** Legacy is not defined by a name engraved on a building or a check written after death. Legacy is the wake your life leaves behind and the effect of your existence on others. You don't build a legacy by accident. You build it daily by choosing integrity over convenience, leading others with love, even when it's hard, and sharing your failures as lessons.

Passing on wisdom, not just wealth, living in such a way that people feel braver, stronger, and more hopeful because of you, drives your passion. When you align your gift with the service of others, your life becomes a conduit for meaning.

Legacy is the Premium Result of Self-Mastery

Most people think self-mastery is only about control over emotions, habits and discipline. But that's only part of the journey. The final layer is transcendence, when you no longer live for your own success, but for the elevation of others. This is why the wisest among us speak more about significance than success. Because mastery without contribution is empty, and when you contribute by teaching, serving, guiding, and uplifting, you tap into the divine.

Practical Daily Legacy Habits

- Mentor someone younger. Share what you wish someone had told you.

- Document your principles. Write down what you believe and why.

- Be consistent. Your example is often more powerful than your words.

- Choose impact over ego by asking, "How can I help?" more than, "How do I look?"

- Practice presence as your undivided attention is one of the greatest gifts you can offer.

Coach John Wooden is often celebrated for his unparalleled record: 10 NCAA championships in 12 years. But Wooden's true legacy is not found in banners or trophies; it's in the generations of leaders, coaches, and citizens shaped by his influence. Wooden's approach to mastery was never just about winning. He believed that character, discipline, and selfless service outlasted any scoreboard. His "Pyramid of Success" emphasized values like industriousness, loyalty, cooperation, and integrity, lessons he modeled every day. Wooden saw coaching not as control, but as contribution: He poured his wisdom, discipline, and love into his players, teaching them to become men of character before champions on the court. The most visible result? His "coaching tree."

Dozens of his former players and assistants, like Kareem Abdul-Jabbar (who became not just an NBA legend but a respected thinker and activist), Bill Walton, and many others, carried his lessons into every arena of life. They became coaches, mentors, teachers, and leaders, passing on Wooden's principles to thousands more.

Each person who benefited from Wooden's guidance went on to influence others, creating a ripple effect that continues to shape basketball, education, and character development worldwide. Wooden's greatest proof of inner strength was not the control he exercised on the sidelines, but the contribution he made through every relationship, every practice, every lesson. His focus shifted from "me" to "we," from achievement to significance.

The Result of Legacy: Wooden's life proves that when mastery overflows into service, your impact outlives your presence. His wisdom became a light for others to follow. Today, thousands of coaches at every level cite John Wooden's teachings as their guiding star, not because of his wins, but because of his values and generosity. He is remembered not just for what he achieved, but for what he gave away. You know you've reached true self-mastery not when you stand alone at the top, but when you see your wisdom, courage, and compassion alive in others.

Legacy is not a monument, but a movement and a living wake that turns your gifts into a better future for those you touch. Proof of inner strength is not control, but contribution. True mastery transcends self and becomes a light others can follow. John Wooden's story is living proof that greatness multiplies through legacy, one life, one lesson and one person at a time.

Tactical Tool: The Legacy Activation Protocol

The climb to self-mastery begins with building yourself, but it ends with building others. True mastery isn't measured by how much you control but by how much you contribute. Impact, not applause, is the currency that endures. Five questions to move from success to significance:

1. Who am I actively helping with the lessons I've already learned?

2. What am I building that will outlive my lifetime?

3. Where can my story give someone else hope?

4. How can I choose significance over status today?

5. If my influence ended tomorrow, what would remain?

Chapter 25
The Blessing of Mastery

When you rule yourself, you become the kind of person life trusts with more. Once again, no one will remember how many likes you had, how fast your car was, or how much you were worth on paper. But they will remember how you made them feel, your courage, your kindness and your conviction.

In the end, it's not about the trophies you collect but the lives you touch. True self-mastery is not about retreating into isolation but rising into service. The highest form of discipline is to become the kind of person whose presence calms storms, whose words build bridges, and whose life gives others permission to rise. That's the summit, when your inner work overflows into the outer world.

Remember, you are here to grow in wisdom, govern your soul, live with fierce clarity, and love with unshakable integrity. Every trial you've faced, wound you've healed, and every truth you've owned has shaped you into someone the world needs.

From a purely investment standpoint, if I could sit across from you right now, heart to heart, soul to soul, I'd tell you this - the greatest return you'll ever receive doesn't come from a stock, a startup, or a piece of real estate. It comes from who you become.

Self-mastery is the decision to take ownership of your life instead of skating by on luck, distraction or fear. Most people are waiting for external changes like more money, a new job, a better partner, but nothing will change until you do. Things won't grow around you until something grows within you. Why is this the best investment? Because you are the common denominator in every area of your life. Your mind goes with you into every relationship, every opportunity, and every challenge. When you strengthen that mind, clarify your values and master your habits, suddenly, your entire life rises to meet you. Consider the ROI:

- A clearer mind makes better decisions.

- A disciplined body builds confidence.

- A refined character earns trust and admiration.

- A calm nervous system becomes your anchor in chaos.

- A purposeful soul is immune to distraction and defeat.

No loss that can steal the wisdom you've earned. That's why this investment never depreciates. It compounds, in peace, relationships, influence and in fulfillment. If you don't invest in your personal growth, you'll pay for it in other ways, like regret, stagnation, bitterness and in wondering, "What could I have become if I had really tried?" Begin now, don't wait for the perfect time. Start where it hurts, or even unclear, but start with everything you've got.

When you bet on your own growth, you're not just investing in a better life; you're investing in a better you. That version of you will know exactly how to create the life you were meant to lead. Live with urgency but not panic, and purpose but not pride. Let your days be guided by alignment.

One day, someone you've never met will be stronger because of how you lived. That is the quiet power of a life well-mastered. And when the final breath comes, you will not fear it, you will greet it like an old friend, for you will have lived on purpose with peace, and for others. Legacy is not what you leave for people, but leave in them. Master yourself so fully that your life becomes a blessing to the world.

When Cyrus the Great of Persia conquered Babylon in 539 BCE, he was able to rule by fear, as most kings of his time did. Instead, he set a precedent almost unheard of in ancient warfare; he freed the captives, restored displaced peoples to their homelands, and even funded the rebuilding of temples, including the Jewish Temple in Jerusalem.

Cyrus's self-mastery lay in his ability to rise above ego and vengeance, seeing that stability and loyalty came from respect rather than terror. The blessing of this restraint was the loyalty of his subjects across vast and diverse lands, creating an empire that endured long after his death and earning him a reputation as one of history's most enlightened rulers.

Tactical Tool: The Self as Your Greatest Asset

Every choice, relationship, and opportunity in your life is filtered through one thing…you. Strengthen that, and everything rises. Neglect it, and everything suffers. Your growth isn't an optional luxury, but the engine that drives all results. Your portfolio might build wealth, but your personal mastery builds legacy. When you grow yourself, you grow everything connected to you. Five questions to keep your growth compounding:

1. If everything I own disappeared tomorrow, what part of me would remain unshaken?

2. Am I building habits today that my future self will thank me for or regret?

3. How do I want people to describe my character when I'm not in the room?

4. Where am I tolerating mediocrity in myself that I wouldn't accept from others?

5. If my life were an investment, am I adding value daily or letting it depreciate?

Responsibilities Review

Your Impact: As personal ascent takes place, the mission shifts from survival to success, to excellence and finally to service. At its highest tier, self-mastery turns surplus into support, where your decisions reach beyond private wins and reverberate through families, teams, and future strangers. You begin asking sharper questions, such as who benefits because I'm here, what work will outlast me, and what will my name mean when I'm gone. Contribution is a targeted impact that offers your skills, lessons, and scars to shorten someone else's struggle.

Self-Mastery Dividends: Real mastery doesn't hide from the world because it overflows into it, becoming a presence that settles internal storms, a voice that builds crossings, and a life that gives others permission to climb.

The wisest and most fruitful investment is upgrading you because your outcomes will rise, compounding into your peace, trust, impact, and deep fulfillment, and in time, your quiet consistency will seed courage in people you'll never meet, and your legacy will be written not on plaques but in the lives you helped lift.

Parting Thoughts

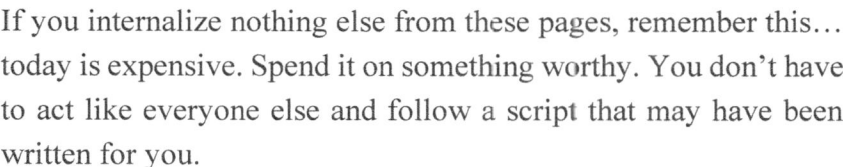

If you internalize nothing else from these pages, remember this... today is expensive. Spend it on something worthy. You don't have to act like everyone else and follow a script that may have been written for you.

Unfortunately, most people trade their dreams and their freedom for someone else's approval. You were born to create, build and express the unique vision only you carry. The world needs the authentic and courageous you, not another copy. Step fearlessly into the unknown with big dreams and take risks.

There is a ruthless law at the heart of self-mastery...either increase your sacrifice or reduce your desires. It's insanity to want or desire more than you are willing to sacrifice for. If you want the next level in self-mastery, and trust me, you owe it to the cosmos to do so, pay the price by spending time in the trenches, having attention without distraction, incorporating humility as you will learn faster than with pride, make discipline outlast mood and don't leave a yard sale of regrets. If you choose to refuse the price, then you can only be content by refusing the fantasy. Freedom begins where self-deception ends, and as a result, you must guard the gates of your mind with the vigilance of a sentinel. The assassins of growth work from the inside:

Laziness kills ambition.
Anger kills wisdom.
Ego kills growth.

161

Jealousy kills peace.
Doubt kills confidence.
Fear kills dreams.

When you feel the pull to drift, return to the question that cuts through fog: What is the cost of inaction right now? Let your life be a ledger of courageous decisions, those moments when you walked past comfort and chose the hard thing that made you real. Let your craft, whatever it may be, carry your signature. Let your relationships feel your integrity, your words be few, and your actions be abundant. Become the person your future wants to meet. That is Glorious Lethal Euphoria.

Glorious Lethal Euphoria
Daily Affirmation

—————◆—————

Today, I refuse to live on autopilot.

I remember the miracle of my existence.

I was born impossible.

I will not waste this day chasing comfort, approval, or distraction.

I will train my mind.

I will lead my emotions.

I will guard my circle.

I will speak with precision.

I will act with courage.

I do not control the world. But I control myself.

When fear speaks, I answer with movement.

When doubt rises, I answer with truth.

When chaos hits, I remain unshaken.

This is my one shot. I will not drift.

I am the master of my mind.

I am the fire behind the words.

I am Glorious. I am Lethal. I am Euphoria.

Enduring Wisdom

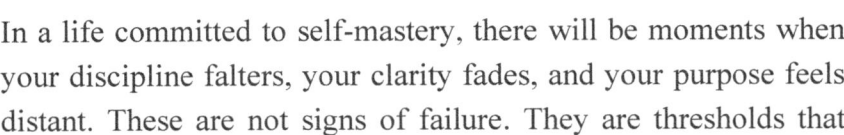

In a life committed to self-mastery, there will be moments when your discipline falters, your clarity fades, and your purpose feels distant. These are not signs of failure. They are thresholds that separate who you were from who you're becoming.

In those moments, words become weapons. Ideas become anchors. And clarity becomes your edge. This collection of quotes, the unfiltered voices of truth-tellers and warriors of the soul, is not meant to impress you. They are meant to arm you, as these lines are more than intellectual ornaments. They are tools...

- For anchoring you when you're lost in emotion

- For humbling you when ego creeps in

- For sharpening you when growth feels dull or distant

- For reminding you of your strength, your freedom, and your responsibility.

You won't need all of them all the time. But you will need the right one at the right time. When that moment comes, whether you're facing betrayal, stagnation, temptation, confusion, or grief, flip to this guide and read until something clicks. Then return to the fight renewed because self-mastery isn't a destination. It's a relentless act of remembering who you truly are, one decision at a time.

On Control, Choice, & Acceptance

- "You have power over your mind, not outside events. Realize this, and you will find strength." —*Marcus Aurelius.*

- "It's not what happens to you, but how you react to it that matters." —*Epictetus.*

- "Fate leads the willing and drags along the reluctant." —*Seneca*

- "Don't demand that things happen as you wish, but wish that they happen as they do, and you will go on well." —*Epictetus*

- "The chief task in life is simply this: to identify and separate matters . . . which are externals not under my control, and which have to do with the choices I actually control." —*Epictetus*

- "Everything can be taken from a man but one thing: the last of human freedoms—to choose one's attitude in any given set of circumstances." —*Viktor Frankl*

- "Between stimulus and response, there is a space. In that space is our power to choose our response." —*Viktor Frankl*

- "Accept—then act. Whatever the present moment contains, accept it as if you had chosen it." —*Eckhart Tolle*

- "The primary cause of unhappiness is never the situation but your thoughts about it." —*Eckhart Tolle*

- "Trust in the Lord with all your heart and lean not on your own understanding." —*Proverbs 3:5*

- "Freedom is the only worthy goal in life. It is won by disregarding things that lie beyond our control." — *Epictetus*

- "He is a wise man who does not grieve for the things which he has not but rejoices for those which he has." —*Epictetus*

- "Nothing is worth doing pointlessly. But life is only pointless if you make it so." —*Marcus Aurelius*

- "Let us train our minds to desire what the situation demands." —*Seneca*

On Adversity, Suffering, & Resilience

- "Difficulties strengthen the mind, as labor does the body." —*Seneca*

- "The impediment to action advances action. What stands in the way becomes the way." —*Marcus Aurelius*

- "Fire tests gold, suffering tests brave men." —*Seneca*

- "When we are no longer able to change a situation, we are challenged to change ourselves." — *Viktor Frankl*

- "Suffering ceases to be suffering at the moment it finds a meaning." — *Viktor Frankl*

- "What is to give light must endure burning." — *Viktor Frankl*

- "Suffering is necessary until you realize it is unnecessary." —*Eckhart Tolle*

- "In much wisdom is much grief, and increased knowledge brings increased sorrow." —*Ecclesiastes 1:18*

- "To be tested is good. The challenged life may be the best therapist." —*Gail Sheehy*

- "The wound is the place where the Light enters you." — *Rumi*

- "Out of suffering have emerged the strongest souls; the most massive characters are seared with scars." —*Khalil Gibran*

- "The world breaks everyone, and afterward many are strong at the broken places." —*Ernest Hemingway*

- "If it doesn't scare you, it won't change you" - *Unknown*

On Presence, Time, & the Now

- "Do not act as if you were going to live ten thousand years. Death hangs over you." —*Marcus Aurelius.*

- "True happiness is to enjoy the present, without anxious dependence upon the future." —*Seneca.*

- "Life is very short and anxious for those who forget the past, neglect the present, and fear the future." —*Seneca.*

- "Realize deeply that the present moment is all you ever have." —*Eckhart Tolle*

- "Wherever you are, be there totally." — *Eckhart Tolle*

- "Stillness is where creativity and solutions to problems are found." — *Eckhart Tolle*

- "Time isn't precious at all . . . what is precious is the one point that is out of time: the Now." — *Eckhart Tolle*

- "The past has no power over the present moment." — *Eckhart Tolle*

- "So I commend the enjoyment of life . . . to eat and drink and be glad." —*Ecclesiastes 8:15*

- "A cheerful heart is good medicine, but a crushed spirit dries up the bones." —*Proverbs 17:22*

- "Forever is composed of nows." —*Emily Dickinson*

- "You must live in the present, launch yourself on every wave, find your eternity in each moment." —*Henry David Thoreau.*

- "Do every act of your life as though it were the very last act of your life." —*Marcus Aurelius*

- "The clock is running. Make the most of today." —*Og Mandino*

- "Your Days decide your decades. A wasted morning compounds into a wasted life" - *Unknown*

- "To the mind that is still, the whole universe surrenders." — *Lao Tzu*

On Character, Virtue, & Discipline

- "Waste no more time arguing what a good man should be. Be one." —*Marcus Aurelius.*

- "No man is free who is not master of himself." —*Epictetus*

- "He who is brave is free." —*Seneca*

- "First say to yourself what you would be; and then do what you have to do." —*Epictetus.*

- "A human being is a deciding being." —*Viktor Frankl*

- "Man conquers the world by conquering himself." —*Zeno of Citium*

- "Iron sharpens iron, so one person sharpens another." —*Proverbs 27:17*

- "Commit your works to the Lord, and your thoughts will be established." —*Proverbs 16:3*

- "We are what we repeatedly do. Excellence, then, is not an act, but a habit." —*Will Durant (summarizing Aristotle)*

- "Discipline is the bridge between goals and accomplishment." —*Jim Rohn*

- "Integrity is doing the right thing, even when no one is watching." —*C.S. Lewis*

- "To live a good life: We have the potential for it. If we learn to be indifferent to what makes no difference." —*Marcus Aurelius*

- "Nothing transforms life faster than decisions followed by constant effort."-*Unknown*

On Wisdom, Perspective, & Ego

- "When you are about to undertake some action, remind yourself of the nature of the action." —*Epictetus.*

- "Everything we hear is an opinion, not a fact. Everything we see is a perspective, not the truth." —*Marcus Aurelius.*

- "We suffer more often in imagination than in reality." —*Seneca*

- "To understand the true quality of people, you must look into their minds." —*Marcus Aurelius*

- "He who laughs at himself never runs out of things to laugh at." —*Epictetus*

- "You are not the voice in your head, but the one who is aware of it." —*Eckhart Tolle*

- "All problems are illusions of the mind." —*Eckhart Tolle*

- "The ego says: I shouldn't have to suffer, and that thought makes you suffer so much more." — *Eckhart Tolle*

- "Pride goes before destruction, and a haughty spirit before a fall." —*Proverbs 16:18*

- "Wisdom is better than weapons of war, but one sinner destroys much good." —*Ecclesiastes 9:18*

- "The most powerful alarm clock is purpose." - *Unknown*

- "Humility is not thinking less of yourself but thinking of yourself less." —*C.S. Lewis*

- "Don't speak ill of others in front of people, as people change their opinion of you, not them"- *Unknown*

- "Clarity about what matters provides clarity about what does not." —*Cal Newport*

- "Some people are so poor, all they have is money"—*Patrick Meagher*

- "Have more than thou show and speak less than thou know"—*William Shakespeare*

On Death, Impermanence, & Legacy

- "You are a little soul carrying around a corpse." —*Epictetus*

- "You could leave life right now. Let that determine what you do and say and think." —*Marcus Aurelius*

- "It is not death that a man should fear but never beginning to live." —*Marcus Aurelius*

- "Life is like a play; it's not the length, but the excellence of the acting that matters." —*Seneca*

- "What you have experienced, no power on earth can take from you." —*Viktor Frankl*

- "He has made everything beautiful in its time." —*Ecclesiastes 3:11*

- "Remember your Creator in the days of your youth." —*Ecclesiastes 12:1*

- "Now all has been heard: Fear God and keep His commandments; for this is the duty of all mankind." —*Ecclesiastes 12:13*

- "The fear of death follows from the fear of life. A man who lives fully is prepared to die at any time." —*Mark Twain*

- "Live as if you were to die tomorrow. Learn as if you were to live forever." —Mahatma Gandhi

- "Our death is not an end if we can live on in our children and the younger generation." —*Albert Einstein*

- "Carve your name on hearts, not tombstones." —*Shannon L. Alder*

On Purpose, Meaning, & Fulfillment

- "Those who have a 'why' to live, can bear with almost any 'how.' "—*Viktor Frankl (via Nietzsche)*

- "Life is never made unbearable by circumstances, but only by lack of meaning." —*Viktor Frankl.*

- "Ultimately, man should not ask what the meaning of his life is but recognize that he is being asked." —*Viktor Frankl.*

- "Success, like happiness, cannot be pursued; it must ensue . . . as the unintended side effect of personal dedication." —*Viktor Frankl.*

- "The more one forgets himself—by giving to a cause or to love—the more human he is." —*Viktor Frankl.*

- "Better a little with righteousness than much gain with injustice." —*Proverbs 16:8*

- "Better a little with the fear of the Lord than great wealth with turmoil." —*Proverbs 15:16*

- "Success is not the key to happiness. Happiness is the key to success. If you love what you are doing, you will be successful." —*Albert Schweitzer.*

Self-Mastery

- "No man is free who is not master of himself." — *Epictetus*

- "Man conquers the world by conquering himself." — *Zeno of Citium*

- "He who is brave is free." —*Seneca*

- "First say to yourself what you would be; and then do what you have to do." —*Epictetus.*

- "You have power over your mind, not outside events. Realize this, and you will find strength." —*Marcus Aurelius.*

- "Everything can be taken from a man but one thing; the last of human freedoms—to choose one's attitude in any given set of circumstances." —*Viktor Frankl.*

- "The primary cause of unhappiness is never the situation but your thoughts about it." —*Eckhart Tolle.*

- "The wise man is his own best friend." —*Seneca.*

- "You are not the voice in your head, but the one who is aware of it." —*Eckhart Tolle.*

- "Waste no more time arguing about what a good man should be. Be one." —*Marcus Aurelius.*

- "Rule your mind or it will rule you." —*Horace*

- "The greatest victory is over self." —*Aristotle*

- "Mastering others is strength; mastering yourself is true power." —*Lao Tzu*

- "Self-control is strength. Right thought is mastery. Calmness is power." —*James Allen*

- "In the end, mastery is the art of becoming the best version of yourself, fueled by deep practice and self-discipline." —*Robert Greene*

Anyone can win a fight, build an empire, or gain influence, but the person who can govern their own heart, responses, and instincts has achieved a rarer, higher victory.

Your Glorious, Lethal Euphoria
Reading Journey

———————— ◈ ————————

The path doesn't end here. You've walked through the fire with *Glorious Lethal Euphoria*. You've challenged your comfort, confronted your fear, and reclaimed the sovereignty of your own mind. But mastery is not a finish line; it's a lifelong climb. The books below aren't just "more reading." They're battle-tested wisdom and philosophical allies that will sharpen, deepen, and extend what you've built here. Let each layer be on the last. Carry the lessons forward, test them against your own life, and pass them on.

Man's Search for Meaning—Viktor E. Frankl

The Obstacle Is the Way—Ryan Holiday

Meditations—Marcus Aurelius

Ecclesiastes—King Solomon

Proverbs—King Solomon

Letters from a Stoic—Seneca

Atomic Habits—James Clear

The Power of Now—Eckhart Tolle

The Psychology of Persuasion—Robert Cialdini

Lifetime of Observations and Reflections—John Wooden

21 Irrefutable Laws of Leadership—John C. Maxwell

What Every BODY Is Saying—Joe Navarro

Can't Hurt Me—David Goggins

48 Laws of Power—Robert Greene

You are not just a reader of these books; you are a builder and participant of philosophy, a practitioner of an uncommon way of living. Every chapter you read from here on out is another weapon in your arsenal, another layer of steel in your soul.

www.ingramcontent.com/pod-product-compliance
Lightning Source LLC
Chambersburg PA
CBHW051156120626
46547CB00012B/1089